THE UNOFFICIAL STORY

living THE DREAM

HannaH MONTana and miley CYrUS

ECW PRESS

Copyright © ECW Press, 2008

Published by ECW Press, 2120 Queen Street East, Suite 200, Toronto, Ontario, Canada M4E 1E2
416.694.3348 / info@ecwpress.com

LIBRARY AND ARCHIVES CANADA CATALOGUING IN PUBLICATION

Janic, Susan
Living the dream: Hannah Montana and Miley Cyrus, the unofficial story / Susan Janic.
ISBN 978-1-55022-848-9
1. Cyrus, Miley, 1992– — Juvenile literature. 2. Singers — United States — Biography — Juvenile literature. 3. Actresses — United States — Biography — Juvenile literature. 4. Hannah Montana (Television program). I. Title.
ML3930.C97J33 2008   782.42164092   C2008-901977-6

Courtesy PicturePerfect/The Canadian Press: 5; Harris McClary/Retna: 6; Marissa Roth/Retna: 7 (right), 30; Bob D'Amico/© Disney/Courtesy Everett Collection/The Canadian Press: 11, 13, 53, 59, 64; © Disney Channel/Courtesy Everett Collection/The Canadian Press: 15, 19, 109, 119; AP Photo/Jennifer Graylock: 16; Jon McKee Photo/Retna: 17; © PA Photos Limited/The Canadian Press: 20; Alex Blasquez/Retna: 21; Jody Cortes/Shooting Star: 23, 75; Mary Leahy: 25, 45, 46, 49, 51, 63, 67; AP Photo/Mark Humphrey: 27; Carol Kaelson/© ABC/Courtesy Everett Collection/The Canadian Press: 29; Sthanlee Mirador/Shooting Star: 31, 39, 44, 77; Ron Galella/WireImage: 32; Tony DiMaio/Shooting Star: 33, 42, 65; AP Photo/Universal Family Entertainment: 35; Sue Schneider/MGP Agency: 36, 50, 52, 122, 133, 141; Christopher Voelker/Shooting Star: 37; Christina Radish: 38, 96, 112; AP Photo/Chris Pizzello: 41, 56; Peter Brooker/Rex Features/The Canadian Press: 43; Mark Sullivan/WireImage: 47; AP Photo/Amanda Parks: 55; Rena Durham/Retna: 57; Ida Mae Astute/© ABC/Courtesy Everett Collection/The Canadian Press: 61, 100; AP Photo/Phelan M. Ebenhack/The Canadian Press: 66; George Taylor/Everett Collection/The Canadian Press: 69; AP Photo/Jeff Christensen/The Canadian Press: 70; Kristin Callahan/Everett Collection/The Canadian Press: 71; Adam Orchon/Everett Collection/The Canadian Press: 72; John Medina/WireImage: 73; Jay Blakesberg: 79, 84, 144; Jim Watson: 80 (left), 83 (second row right, bottom left photos); Jennifer H: 80 (right), 81, 82, 83 (bottom left corner), 104, 106; Corrin Marie: 83 (top row, second row left); Dara Kushner/INFGoff.com/The Canadian Press: 85; Sebastian Artz/Retna: 86; Grant/X17online.com/The Canadian Press: 87; Marc Morrison/Retna: 88; Yoram Kahana/Shooting Star: 90; Gregg DeGuire/WireImage: 92; AP Photo/Jason DeCrow/The Canadian Press: 93; AP Photo/Mark Duncan: 94; AP Photo/Chitose Suzuki: 95 (left); Jose Perez/INFGoff.com/The Canadian Press: 95 (right); Cristopher McRae: 97; Camera Press/Retna: 98; Patsy Lynch/Rex Features/The Canadian Press: 99; George Taylor/Everett Collection/The Canadian Press: 101; Devan/INFphoto.com/The Canadian Press: 102; © Lionel Hahn/ABACAUSA.com/The Canadian Press: 103; Hugh Thompson/Rex Features/The Canadian Press: 105; AP Photo/Kevork Djansezian: 107; Michael Germana/Everett Collection/The Canadian Press: 113; Tony Rivetti/© Disney Channel/Courtesy Everett Collection/The Canadian Press: 114; Alexandra Wyman/WireImage: 116; Michael Desmond/© Disney Channel/Courtesy Everett Collection/The Canadian Press: 118; Joel Warren/© Disney Channel/Courtesy Everett Collection/The Canadian Press: 125, 127, 128, 131, 135, 137

Editor: Jennifer Hale
Cover, text design, and production: Tania Craan
Cover Images: AP Photo/Damian Dovarganes (Hannah) and The Canadian Press/Kimberly P. Mitchell/Detroit Free Press/MCT/Abacapress.com (Miley)
Printing: Transcontinental

The publication of *Living the Dream* has been generously supported by the Government of Canada through the Book Publishing Industry Development Program (BPIDP).

PRINTED AND BOUND IN CANADA

INTRODUCTION

What is it that makes a phenomenon? What are the key ingredients that result in the perfect storm of circumstances to result in a pop culture sensation? It's a difficult question that could only be answered with uncertainty or else *everything* would be a phenomenon.

But actress/singer Miley Cyrus is that perfect storm. Or maybe it's her dual on-screen Disney Channel personas of Miley Stewart and Hannah Montana. The bottom line is that the stars aligned in such a way that Miley, the daughter of country singer Billy Ray Cyrus, persisted in auditioning for the *Hannah Montana* role, and was consistently turned away but nonetheless kept picking herself up, dusting herself off and trying again. And obviously that persistence paid off. Miley was cast — as a pop superstar who is trying to balance her celebrity with a normal life, thus living a secret identity along the lines of Clark Kent and Superman — and *instantly* connected with the television audience, which turned the character and Miley herself into a sensation.

And since that debut there have been CDs that have sold in the millions, fashion and book lines, best-selling DVDs, a concert tour that sold out literally within seconds of tickets going on sale (with one woman going so far as to spend $13,000 on a set of four tickets!), a 3D concert film and a full-length feature film.

What's most impressive about all of this is the fact that Miley seems so incredibly unaffected by it all. Miley has often expressed her amazement at the speed at which everything has changed, though she has been sure to emphasize that she's still the same person, and that her family dynamic has remained the same. They still go to church as a family every Sunday and hang out together as often as they can. On a personal level, she's filled with inner contentment over the fact that she's finally accomplished her dreams, though at a considerably faster rate than she ever expected.

Well, if the past year is any indication, things are only going to get faster and more intense. But Miley, surrounded by her friends and family, has given every indication that she'll be able to handle everything that comes her way in a style that's all her own. It's what being a phenomenon is all about.

Susan Janic
December 2007

THe real
miley

"I knew that I loved
the entertainment business
enough to keep acting and
singing for the rest of my life."

Miley (far right), her brothers and mom join Billy Ray Cyrus on stage during a Fan Fair fan club party at their home in June 2001

With a name like Destiny Hope, it was inevitable that the girl the world would come to know as Hannah Montana would ultimately be fated for show business greatness. It also didn't hurt that her father was country singer Billy Ray Cyrus, he of "Achy Breaky Heart" fame.

Born on November 23, 1992, in Nashville, Tennessee, to Billy Ray and his wife Leticia "Tish" Cyrus, Miley was given the moniker Destiny Hope out of sheer optimism: her parents felt that she was genuinely destined for great things. Growing up, she was also given the nickname "Smiley" by her parents. "She's just always

been smiling," offers Billy Ray in explanation. "As a little baby, she just had that smile on her face and as you talk to a little baby, it's, like, 'Oh, she's smiling,' and all of a sudden she became Smiley."

"My dad made all these cute poems and all of these things about saying when I was a baby, I used to smile all the time. He used to do this baby talk or whatever and he started dropping letters every now and then, which is how he went from 'Oh, she's smilin' to Miley. And by the time I started grade school, my mom suggested they shorten it to Miley so it wouldn't be embarrassing. I could imagine being fifteen years

old and my dad would be picking me up at school and be yelling, 'Hey, Smiley Miley, get in the car.' So my mom had a point. My grandma is the only one who still calls me Destiny Hope, but my mom and dad love the name Miley and it stuck with me."

Growing up, Miley found herself in a loving family environment — and what a family it was. Besides her parents, there was her older half-brother Christopher, from a previous relationship Billy Ray had been in; older half-sister Brandi and half-brother Trace from a previous relationship of Leticia's; younger brother Braison Chance and younger sister Noah Lindsey.

Over the years, Miley has pointed out that her faith and values were instilled in her at a young age, and that family is one of the most important things to her.

Miley discovered her desire to be part of the entertainment world at a very young age, largely because even as a toddler she became absolutely mesmerized by the response her father got every time he took to the stage. By the age of two or three, she could sense the magic there; a connection between the man she called Dad and the audience that was calling out his name.

"Having a famous dad was kind of cool," she smiles. "That's where I got the

Eight-year-old Miley and actress Sarain Boylan goof around on the set of *Doc*

idea that I wanted to sing and act, because I sang onstage with him. If it wasn't for my dad, I never would have discovered that I love it. I was singing on the stage with my dad when I was two. I would sing 'Hound Dog' and silly songs for the fun of it."

"When she was three," Billy Ray says, "I would be on stage and she was supposed to be off to the side . . ."

Miley interjects, "He says I escaped from my nanny. Occasionally."

"She would *always* escape," he clarifies. "If I was up on stage, singing, performing, if she broke free, she was coming out and getting a hold of that microphone."

Remembers Miley, "It was an Elvis tribute and there were all of these legends there. And my nanny — bless her, I have no idea how she did this — let me escape. I kicked and ran and I went up there and grabbed the microphone and started singing. And they started passing me around. It was so much fun that I would escape whenever I could to try and grab the microphone."

Yet while she was trying to hog the spotlight, she also did her best to hide the

8

identity of her father. "When I was living in Nashville, my hometown, I wouldn't tell them who my dad was, because I wanted to have friends who really loved me for me. To those who knew, I was always Billy Ray Cyrus's daughter . . . never Miley."

Flash forward to today, of course, and the exact opposite is true. Billy Ray smiles, "Miley used to be known as Billy Ray Cyrus's daughter. Now I'm known as Miley Cyrus's father. And I couldn't be happier. I'm just so proud of that little girl."

Early in her life, Miley turned her natural tendency for the spotlight toward cheerleading. Actually, competitive cheerleading, which meant that she traveled all around Tennessee as part of the Tennessee All Stars. "The training is pretty harsh," she admits, "but it's so worth it once you're on stage and getting trophies."

She also loved putting on shows for willing and sometimes not-so-willing audiences. "When I was little, I would stand up on couches and say, 'Watch me!'" she laughs. "We had these showers that are completely glass, and I would lock people in them and make them stay in there and watch me perform. I'd make them watch!"

Ironically, Billy Ray — despite Miley's ease in front of the camera and an audience — would have been thrilled if his daughter had stayed with cheerleading. He knew that being a star had its disadvantages. He had, after all, experienced meteoric heights with the success of his song "Achy Breaky Heart," and then the depths of a fickle public "moving on."

"I tried to discourage Miley from pursuing the entertainment business, because it's a double-edged sword. For everything that makes you happy, there's something equally heartbreaking. I told her, 'You don't want to be a part of this business,'" he reflects. "There are things you can do that are less abusive. I would say, 'Hey, why don't you just be a kid for a while, enjoy school, enjoy cheerleading, take some time off from auditions for a while?' She wouldn't even hear that. She'd say, 'I have one next week.' She was always very serious about it and I'm very proud of her that she would set a goal and not stop. I mean, from the day she could talk she said she was going to be on stage. She was going to be a movie star, a singer, a songwriter, an entertainer."

Unable to convince her otherwise, Billy Ray got behind Miley, who offers, "My dad's motto is if you're not having fun, it ain't working. He says you should always be loving what you're doing, and it's paid off. I'm having a great time. There's just something about it I really love. At first it was like an after-school hobby, but then I started getting into it. I get to do everything I want to do. For a little while I just wanted to be a dancer. For a little while I wanted to be a singer. For a little while I wanted to be an actress. Now I do it all."

The road to doing it all began when Miley auditioned for and got her first role in 2003 when she was cast as "Young Ruthie" in director Tim Burton's fanciful film *Big Fish*. Although it was a small part, it was nonetheless a start and opened a whole new world to Miley.

That same year she also scored a role in the music video for Rhonda Vincent's "If Heartaches Have Wings," and appeared with her father on *Colgate Country Showdown*, which Billy Ray was hosting. But it was when the family temporarily relocated to Toronto for the shooting of Billy Ray's drama series *Doc* that things began to crystallize for her. It was while there that Miley began taking acting lessons, made several guest appearances on the show and started the long audition process that would ultimately change her life forever.

"By that time," Miley reflects, "I knew that I loved the entertainment business enough to keep acting and singing for the rest of my life."

The real test was yet to come.

THE WORLD OF
HANNAH MONTANA

By the time TV critics from around the country had gathered together for the annual Television Critics Association confab — a means for the networks and cable channels to introduce their new programs and stars to the world — the Disney Channel's *Hannah Montana* had already proven itself to be one of the Mouse House's biggest hits. Which wasn't entirely surprising to Disney Channel President of Entertainment Gary Marsh, who muses, "Having a secret identity is a private fantasy for lots of kids. There are lots of shows about boys with a secret identity, but no one's really created that same kind of wish-fulfillment fantasy for girls, until now."

As publicist Patti McTeague noted to those gathered for the International Press Tour event — taking place on the show's sets — *Hannah Montana* premiered on March 24, 2006, to the highest ratings for any kid-targeted channel since 1999 for any series premiere. "That's 5.4 million viewers," she emphasized. "And in the last six weeks, it's created quite a storm. We get very happy phone calls every Monday morning about the ratings. I've never seen anything take off so well in the mainstream press, either. It was created by Michael Poryes, who brought us another smash hit called *That's So Raven*. He is our executive producer, along with Steve Peterman, who is a two-time Emmy Award winner for his work on *Murphy Brown* and, previously, *Suddenly Susan*."

Poryes got his start as a writer for episodic television back in the 1970s, when he began scoring gigs on such shows as *Alice, The Facts of Life, Small Wonder, The Fall Guy, Who's the Boss, Saved By the Bell, Roseanne* and *Me and the Boys*. In 1997 he served as executive producer of *Veronica's Closet* and co-executive producer of *Cybill*. These eventually led him to create the aforementioned *That's So Raven* and, of course, *Hannah Montana*.

Peterman began his career as an actor, appearing in a number of shows in single guest spots, although he was a recurring character on the legal drama *The Paper Chase*. He moved into writing, penning an episode of *A Different World*, which was followed by him serving as supervising producer of *Murphy Brown*, executive producer and "developer" of *Suddenly Susan*, co-executive producer of *Becker* and executive producer of *Hannah Montana*.

As is obvious from their collective credits, Poryes and Peterman had spent most of their careers writing for primetime *adult* sitcoms and the question was whether or not they would have to take a radically different approach in writing a show designed for kids.

"I was very confident," admits Poryes. "I have a ten-year-old boy and one of the biggest thrills about writing this kind of show, is that I can go home and talk stories with my son. He reads the scripts. He can come to the tapings, unlike when he couldn't come to *Cybill* and *Veronica's Closet* and things like that. You really have an opportunity to write a show that you want your kid to watch that you don't have to feel like you need to be in the room to watch with them to make sure it's alright. He's going to laugh. It's going to be a nice journey. It's going to be about something. So writing in this marketplace, for me, is really the biggest thrill of my career because of my son. And because it allows me to tap in and just have a unique relationship with him as a parent."

"It's the same for me," adds Peterman. "My son is now fourteen. He comes to the show almost every week. He hangs out with me down by the monitors. He helps our catering guys serve pizza to the audience during the show. He loves being a part of it. He says it's a great place to meet girls. And

when I was doing *Murphy Brown*, he was in a stroller. He doesn't really remember it. Like Michael's son, he's a great soundboard. We show our kids our rough cuts, we run ideas past them. And Michael and I both felt the show would be huge. It was such a powerful hook and we had the right cast. We've all been on shows where the writing can be as great as possible and if you don't have the right chemistry on that stage, it doesn't matter.

"Part of our confidence came from the fact that my son was laughing at it," he continues. "My son does not watch Disney. He's older. He watches other stuff, but he said, 'This is pretty good.' I told the guys from Disney and they said, 'Well, he's your kid. He has to say nice stuff.' And I said, 'You don't know my kid. You don't know what kids are like.' When I do a bad joke, he'll say, 'Well, that's why you're working for Disney.' He can be brutal. It's no different than prime time — the emotions, the things that people want in life, don't change. I think the only thing that changes is your sophistication in the way you express what you want, or what you're trying to get, or your frustration at not being able to get it. The emotions are just the same, you just try to shift your gear down to remember how you talked about it when you were a kid. You listen to how your kids are talking. We ask the kids sometimes, 'How would you say this? How would this come out of your mouth?' And so they'll help us make sure that it does feel right."

Poryes emphasizes, "And our audience is kids, and there are more constraints on what you have to do. It's like stand-up comedy guys not being able to use profanity. You have to get your humor more purely out of the character and out of real life and out of situations and you can't go to the easy jokes. In that way, Steve and I think it's challenging and it's fun. The bottom line is you know you have good characters when kids go, 'Boy, wouldn't it be nice to hang out with them one day?' That's the secret, really, to the Disney Channel and what I believe makes them different from Nickelodeon. They're about the funny, but we're more about the reality and the truth, what kids really go through: 'My friend is going to be dumped by this guy. What am I going to do?'"

"When we look at the prime time market now," says Peterman, "both Michael and I have worked on some really lovely shows in the past, but I don't see a lot out there that I'm rushing to write. It's a different time and the market is very segmented. There aren't the kind of shows that I liked when I was working a few years ago. As Michael says, there is something so rewarding about doing a show that matters so much to its audience. We get that from friends of the family, you see it in the faces of the kids when they come to see the show. This show matters to them in a way that was really kind of exciting for us and makes us feel like we have a certain responsibility to do the kind of show, like Michael was saying, that we would want our kids to watch."

Which, naturally, leads to the question of just where the concept for *Hannah Montana* — probably one of the most unique and interesting ideas to come along for a series in a long time — came from.

"About a year and a half ago, my writing partner, Gary Dontzig, and I were brought in by Disney to look at a script that Michael Poryes had written about a teenage girl who is a rock star, but wants a little bit of a normal life, so she goes to school incognito and nobody knows who she is," Peterman details. "We fell in love with the story for a bunch of reasons. First of all, everybody — as least as far as I know — at some time in their life wants to be a rock and roll star. I had a band in high school, some of you may have been in bands or played air guitar. I

loved that story. But what I also loved about it was Michael created a girl who knew that being a celebrity was great, but what was most important in life was your family and your friends; the people who really care about you. My son watches *American Idol* and dreams about being a celebrity, like a lot of American kids do. I loved the message of this show, which is, celebrity's great, but don't forget what really matters in life."

Peterman and Dontzig set about rewriting Poryes' script, simplifying a few things and merging a couple of characters. "And," Peterman smiles, "in the timeless tradition of *Bambi* and *The Lion King*, decided, well, one parent should probably be dead. Disney didn't mind. It made the show a little cheaper to do. Then we started our search, because we agreed with Disney: this show didn't work unless you really had a Hannah Montana. They looked all over the country and all over the world, really, to try and find the girl to play this part. And there was one girl we kept coming back to. We saw the tape of this skinny little stick of a girl from Tennessee, with this amazing face and these incredible eyes. She was green and inexperienced. She had done one little part in a movie called *Big Fish* down in Tennessee, but there was something about her face; you couldn't take your eyes off her. There was a wonderful transparency; a sense of a young girl wanting desperately to be something."

Notes Disney Channel Entertainment President Gary Marsh, "In Miley we saw a girl who has this natural ebullience. She loves every minute of her life. It shows in her demeanor and performance. What nailed it is that she sang for us in a conference room in front of fifteen people. That was the first moment it crystallized that she was the 'it' girl."

It was the confidence that she exuded that impressed everyone, as well as the fact that she reminded them of a teenage Lucille Ball and that she had a singing voice well beyond her young years.

"I auditioned forever, and the audition process for anything is so scary," Miley recalls. "You walk into a room with sixty girls. You can see their head shots and just know they know a lot more than you do. And then people you're auditioning for don't like you, which is the scariest part! At first they said I was too small and too young. I was there from the beginning stages, but I was not in their mind for Hannah. I was auditioning for Lilly [which ultimately went to Emily Osment]. It was crazy. I was eleven and it was a fifteen-year-old part, so no way that I looked right. But I kept auditioning. I didn't even know who was producing it, I just loved the script and it really related to me and a lot of other girls. It was definitely a long process. It was hard to hit the nail on the head. I was so sad. I was, like, 'Well, why would you even have me try again?' But they did, so I was saying to myself, 'They're gonna see how old I can really look, so I'll dress up and wear mama's shoes and makeup,' and I was still too small, too young. I just looked like a little girl playing dress up. I don't think at

"They got the normal, average girl and turned me into a pop star."

the beginning I was quite ready for the part. I don't know that *I* would've hired me at that point. But I'm glad they waited."

In truth, Miley almost didn't give them a choice. As Billy Ray recalls, "She was quite determined, diligent and persistent. While I was in Toronto [shooting *Doc*], she found the best coaches, worked on her chops, went to auditions, and did all the different things to reach her goal."

Unfortunately they rejected her a second time, but after a short while she once again requested to be allowed to try again, emphasizing that she would pay for the trip to California herself. Needless to say, it eventually paid off. "We got a call from an agent," reveals Disney's Gary Marsh, "who said, 'Miley will fly herself out to audition again.' Let me tell you, we've done a lot of auditions over the years, and no one has ever made that offer before. I said, 'We have to see this girl again.'"

"We kept coming back to her," says Peterman. "We said, 'She's so young,' and was also about six inches shorter than she is now. We all saw the same thing, but everybody was a little worried. 'What do you think?' 'Is she able to do this?' 'Could she do this?' 'This is going to be an enormous weight on somebody's shoulders.' We brought her out here and we read her and we read her again. We asked her if she would mind singing for us and she basically said, 'You can bring the whole building. I'll sing for everybody.' This little girl opened up her mouth and this amazing voice came out of her that was from somebody twice as big and several years older. And then we realized that Miley Cyrus is the daughter of Billy Ray Cyrus, and those genes are very apparent. So we all took a deep breath. We said to ourselves, 'We can go with someone with more experience, but if we were lucky — if Miley was able to bring out what we saw — we would have something very special.' Because we looked at her with her Tennessee twang and those eyes, that face — there's nobody on TV like this girl. We took the plunge and gave Miley the role."

Explains Marsh, "We said we will not go forward until we can find an actress who can carry a sitcom as well as she can carry a tune. What's amazing about Miley is she's very natural, but completely self-aware. She's precocious, but a complete innocent. She has the everyday relatability of Hilary Duff and the stage presence of Shania Twain. It's a unique combination that enables her to straddle the two worlds she has to as she plays Miley and Hannah."

"It's so awesome," Miley says. "I've never really done anything like this before. I really like it, because it's natural. I don't have to really act too much. And it's definitely something that a lot of girls my age would love to do, because who wouldn't want to be a rock star? I relate to both parts so easily. I take the script in, but it's important to be myself. I didn't want to make a big fake persona, because the script calls for a real girl. So, my being from Tennessee with no

experience worked to my advantage — they got the normal, average girl and turned me into a pop star."

Reported *Variety*, the first real test came when Disney execs staged a Hannah Montana concert at the Alex Theater in Glendale, California. This concert was, according to the magazine, "for a group of 700 unsuspecting tweens who were invited with the promise of a concert and the chance to be on TV. Video of the 'concert' was shown to media buyers at the Disney Channel upfront presentation to advertisers in New York in early February. It's times

"I don't think at the beginning I was quite ready for the part. I don't know that I would've hired me at that point. But I'm glad they waited."

like these that it looks easy. The teens reacted — or else just acted — as if they were meeting the Beatles at Heathrow or at least at a Britney Spears concert. The reaction surprised even young Cyrus, who had had four days with a coach and choreographer to get six songs right. 'It was crazy, because I was expecting dead silence,' Cyrus says. 'They had no idea who Hannah Montana was.'"

Naturally the challenges for Miley didn't stop once she got the part: there was also the fact that she would be playing the dual roles of Miley Stewart and Hannah Montana, and had to create clearly delineated performances for each one to sell the idea that they're two separate people.

"As an actor, it's really fun, because you get to experience different things from different perspectives," she says. "As a person, it's a little harder. It's double the work — not only for me, but for the wardrobe people, the hair and makeup people and everyone else. It's hard, but really fun to be the character. The cool part is I've gotten to add my own take to it."

On screen she's had some fun with that notion of having a "secret identity" as well. "In the boyfriend episode," she points out, "where he tells Miley Stewart he doesn't like Hannah and she stinks, I'm there telling him, 'No, no, she's awesome. You need to go see her. Buy her CD.' You know, all of these great things. And he comes up just to surprise me and says, 'I'm going to take you to a Hannah Montana concert.' And I can't say no, because I've just told him that she's my favorite singer. So I'm there and Lilly and Oliver are there, too, trying to — when I escape to get on stage — distract him. So it's kind of hard, because I'll be in the middle of a scene and I'm like, 'Who am I? Who am I supposed to be? Who was thinking what?' Sometimes that's kind of crazy, but it's really fun 'cause that's kind of what it would be like in real life. Everyone would be saying, 'This is kind of creepy,' you know, two people in the same situation. So that shows the reality of what Hannah Montana goes through."

Had she *not* been cast, Miley would have been equipped to handle that, too, thanks to her father: "My dad always told me that casting agents are like artists picturing their painting in their mind. They know what they want for a role and not to take it too seriously if I don't get the part."

Billy Ray Cyrus

ROBBY STEWART

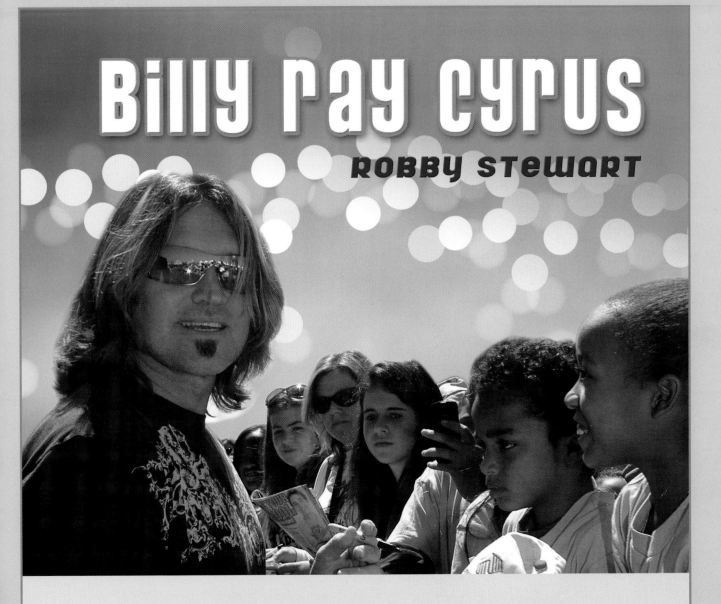

Once the premise for *Hannah Montana* was reshaped and the decision made to have Hannah come from a single parent home due to the death of her mother, the search began for an actor to play Robby Stewart, the singer who had given up his career to nurture his daughter's. Although the producers hadn't initially thought of it, the answer was right under their nose in the form of Miley Cyrus's real-life father, Billy Ray.

"When I left *Doc*, I said I will never do another TV series," says Billy Ray. "I really missed making music and being with my fans. Then this opportunity came up — such a great script, the opportunity to be in business with such a great company like Disney, and then, the icing on the

Billy Ray with cast and crew on the set of *Doc*

cake, to get to work and experience this with my daughter."

Ironically, though, Billy Ray was nowhere near the radar of the producers. "During the casting of Miley," explains Steve Peterman, "Billy Ray had been in the background, terrified and excited for his daughter. Once she had gotten the role, he came to us and said, 'You know, if you guys are open to it, if you wouldn't mind maybe giving me a chance to audition for you.' We had been thinking, 'She's so green. We should probably get someone who's done a lot of comedy.' And Billy, while he's been a performer all of his life, and had done an hour drama show, he was someone we just

weren't sure about. We figured, 'Well, he's the dad. I don't know how we can say no.' So we brought him in to audition. We had another very talented, very professional Los Angeles actor who came in before Billy to read. After he left the room, they'd been sitting out in the lobby together, Billy came in and said, 'You know, you should probably give it to that guy. I think he's really funny.' And we said, 'Well, this is an interesting way to audition for a role.'"

Adds Michael Poryes, "Even before that we were saying, 'We'll have him come in. We'll be polite. We'll listen. We'll let him audition and we'll shake his hand and he'll go away.' Then he came in and he absolutely nailed the role."

Admits Billy Ray, "I was nervous as can be. Miley came in and read the scene with me. Then they sent me out and, you know,

I sat out in the lobby for a little while. And then they called me back in and I read again. And then they sent me away again."

Miley states, "I love working with my dad, so everything has fallen into place, but there was some weird pressure. Like when other actors auditioned to play my father, I'd think, 'I really like him, too. He's so nice.' So it was weird driving home with my dad and he'd be saying he didn't know if he was going to get the job. After a while, I did know he had gotten it, but I couldn't say anything until the producers called him, just in case something happened and they changed their minds."

Eventually, though, Billy Ray found out that he had gotten the part. Says Miley, "They just loved the chemistry between me and my dad. It was great, just awesome."

As Peterman explains it, the key to his success was that he didn't really have to *act* the part of Miley's father. "He *was* Miley's father," the producer laughs. "He approached it with such effortlessness that we said, 'Not only is this her dad, you can't create that, but he is a rock and roller. He *is* the part.' And on top of that, the gravy, the bonus, was that Miley had a relationship to him that you can't duplicate. There was a teasingness, a warmth, a comfort and a security that these two had on stage that we said you could work for years with people and pray to get that kind of a relationship. So we said, 'This is the guy.' Miley acted in a way with her father that she couldn't act with anybody else. Over and over again in the filming of

Billy Ray attends the premiere of *Ratatouille* with his kids Braison, Brandi and Noah Cyrus

the show, some of our favorite moments are things that happen spontaneously between father and daughter that we could never write. And after we had the two of them, everything very quickly fell into place."

Billy Ray Cyrus was born on August 25, 1961, in Flatwoods, Kentucky, to Ron Cyrus (a politician) and his wife, Ruth Ann. As a child, music did *not* serve as a major attraction to him. Instead, he wanted to "be" Cincinnati Reds catcher Johnny Bench, though there was certainly music in his life.

"My earliest memories," he reflected to CNN, "are Saturday nights at my Papo

Casto's house. Papo means grandfather. And so I'd be there and my mom would play the piano and my papo would play fiddle. And my uncle and dad played the guitars, and we'd sing bluegrass — songs like 'Won't You Come Home, Bill Bailey' and 'Roll in My Sweet Baby's Arms.' My other papo was a Pentecostal preacher, so on Saturday nights we'd play bluegrass music and Sunday mornings we'd be in his church where he would preach. And my dad had a gospel quartet called the Crownsmen Quartet. They were very successful in the Kentucky, Ohio, West Virginia realm there. Kind of like the same circuit where my papo would go for these revivals. My dad would do these singings and I'd go with him and we'd sing 'Swing Low, Sweet Chariot,' 'Old Rugged Cross' and 'I'll Fly Away.' It was feel-good music, both the bluegrass and the gospel, southern gospel. And to this very day, that's what I like to do, is make music that moves people."

Largely because he never thought he could play a guitar properly, Billy Ray's dream of being a catcher was still alive — he was even going to school on a baseball scholarship — but he started finding himself drawn to the idea of being a musician, largely because of "all of those nights" with his family and feeling that a voice inside his head was telling him to get his hands on a guitar and start a band. It all came together in his mind when he ended up at a Neil Diamond concert.

"I go to this concert," he detailed, "and I keep hearing this voice saying, 'This is your purpose in life: to make music.' When I went to this concert, I heard Neil Diamond saying, 'You know what? It doesn't matter if you're white or black or rich or poor or a man or a woman. If you believe in your dreams and have faith, you can do anything in this world that you believe you can do.' Right then it's like I had hands on me saying this was my purpose. That voice said I should buy a left-handed guitar. I didn't know there was a difference. I'd been left-handed and left-footed my whole life, but I didn't know there was a difference for right-handed, left-handed guitar players. I went the next day and bought a left-handed guitar and started a band that night and found out that I could play, I just had the guitar upside down."

Billy Ray gave himself ten months to bring his dreams to life. He began writing songs and continually tried to get signed in Nashville. Eventually he moved to Los Angeles, where, in 1990, he secured a recording contract with Mercury Nashville Records. His first album, 1992's *Some Gave All*, spawned the monster single "Achy Breaky Heart," which really put Billy Ray on

"Not only is this her dad, but he is a rock and roller. He is the part."

26

the map. At the time, that song and Billy Ray were *everywhere*, but, unfortunately, he never quite achieved that level of success musically again. He followed with eight additional albums between 1993 and 2007, but, unfortunately, the only one to have some sort of traction on the charts has been the most recent, *Home at Last*, which no doubt has been helped by the success of *Hannah Montana*.

With the encouragement of his father, Billy Ray decided to give acting a try, and surprised himself when he found himself hired for the 1999 independent film *Radical Jack*, which was followed by David Lynch's 2001 production of *Mulholland Drive*. It was Lynch who further encouraged him, emphasizing that Billy Ray could succeed as an actor as long as he kept himself "real" on camera.

"Then I read about this series called *Doc*, and it represented hope and faith and love," he explained. "And I said, 'All right, God, if you want me to be an actor, then tell me what to do.' And the voice said, 'Go to the audition.' I went to the audition and they hired me. Four years and 88 episodes later, I was a full-time actor on *Doc*. It lasted for years and went into syndication. I came back from Toronto and said, 'All right, I'm going to get serious about my music. I'm never going to do another series ever again.' Next thing I know, here comes *Hannah Montana*."

Which in turn led to him being invited to be a contestant on ABC's *Dancing With the Stars*, a gig he took on at the insistence of his kids. Despite both the media and the judges being less than kind to his performances, he decided to make the best of the situation.

"I'm not a dancer," said Billy Ray. "That's a misconception about me. I don't know anything about dancing. But I did it, and on one given night, I look across the dance floor and there's Muhammad Ali. And I said, 'You know what? These judges are going to roast me no matter what I do, so I'm going to go see my hero.' And right at the end of my dance, I went over and kind of squared up, started throwing some punches. And he put that fist up there and threw a couple of punches back. And so while I stood there getting roasted by the judges, he kept throwing those punches. And I was, like, 'Wow, that's Muhammad Ali.' And when we took a break, he came

and gave me a big hug. And that was worth it all for me right there."

But nothing he's accomplished professionally can compare to the thrill he's had working with Miley on *Hannah Montana*. Which is not to say that things were destined to go smoothly. After all, the relationship between parents and their teenage children can often be strained. Naturally, there was a concern that tensions could arise during the course of the series and put a strain on the relationship between Billy Ray and Miley that would far surpass what most people would go through by merely living together. Now father and daughter were living together, commuting together and working together, day after day.

"There are a lot of responsibilities in having a teenage daughter," Billy Ray offers. "It's a very delicate time for a father and a daughter, and then to have a professional relationship. . . . Well, like I said, it's a pretty delicate balance. I don't think there's ever going to be a place where we lock in and say, 'Okay, this is it. This is perfect.' I think it will always be changing. For me, what I'm trying to say is that I see I need to give Miley space. That there are times where I just have to step back and let her do her thing. You'll never hear me give her advice, unless she asks for it.

"The best thing about this relationship," he continues, "is watching her grow and spending time together, watching her evolve as an actress and knowing she didn't just fall into it. She came to Toronto while I

was doing *Doc* and studied very, very diligently with great coaches. She really applied herself to this. She really worked hard to get to this point. For me to be able to see her evolving and growing as an actress and also realizing her dream is very rewarding."

"The best thing about working with my dad is sharing this journey with him and every day just getting to hang out with my best friend all day. It's a lot of fun. If there's anything negative," Miley says with a laugh, "I'd have to say that it's the ride to work each day. He talks the entire way about the most random things I've ever heard in my life, and plays the most random music. I have no idea what it is. I'm, like, 'Yeah, Dad, that's great. Okay.' Finally, I turn on my little iPod and let him talk to himself. I'm like

any other teenage girl who doesn't necessarily want her dad around all the time. You know, I used to go to work with him all the time and now it's like he's going to work with me, which is really weird. It can be really freaky, because sometimes I'll go to school in the morning or whatever, and then all of a sudden my dad will be sitting in my dressing room and it's, like, so weird. But once we get on stage it's really awesome. I would never let him know this, but he's really cool. Overall, though, it's a lot of fun."

But what happens — as silly as this may sound when you're talking about a star as big as she is — when Miley misbehaves and needs discipline? Don't look to Billy Ray. "I've never been good — non-existent, really — with discipline. I've never been able to

spank 'em or command that type of fatherly figure with my children. What I try to do in real life is use psychology, make 'em laugh or tell a story to make a point. That's what Robby does, too."

Peterman points out that if he's learned anything about the Cyrus family, it's that "Billy's already done this before in his life. He's had this experience of becoming very big and he's learned how to handle it. Billy treats everybody on this show, from the people on top to the guy who comes in to clean up, like a member of the family. I think you learn by example. I see that the example that he's setting for his daughter is this is how you treat people. I think it's terrific."

emily osment

lilly TRUSCOTT

Emily with her brother Haley Joel and their parents

One of Miley Stewart's best friends, and one of the very few people who know about her life as Hannah Montana, is Lilly Truscott, a role that ultimately went to actress Emily Osment (younger sister of *The Sixth Sense*'s Haley Joel), though initially the producers weren't exactly sure that Emily herself was truly trying for the part.

"We needed somebody tough and all-American to be Miley's buddy," explains Peterman. "Emily came in with her hands straight down at her sides. I thought, 'I don't know. Does she even want to be here? Is she uncomfortable?'"

"'Is she dead?'" laughs Poryes.

"Then she opened her mouth," Peterman continues, "and she blew us out of the room. I said to my wife at home, 'I think we found our Lilly.' The next day I was at my son's school for a Little League game and I see Emily go tearing past me, chasing somebody on the playground. I stopped her and I said, 'You auditioned for us yesterday. You did a really good job.' She said, 'Oh, thanks. Thanks a lot,' and then she went tearing back off after this kid. At that point I said, 'That's the girl.'"

Recalls Emily, "I remember driving home from school the day I got the part. I screamed for ten minutes. I knew the show would go far, but not this far."

Emily Jordan Osment was born on March 10, 1992, in Los Angeles, California, to her parents, actor Eugene Osment and teacher Theresa. Acting for her was almost an afterthought. "My dad did a lot of theater," she explains, "and so does my brother. I'd see them rehearsing sometimes when I was little and I'd think, 'I want to do

that.' But I think it all started when I was little, when I was five years old. My dad just sort of asked me if I wanted to get into it and I said, 'Yeah, sure, why not?' I mean, I was five years old! I started doing commercials, small TV appearances and then movies, and now the show. I think it all just builds up to this, and it took a lot of years, but here I am."

Emily's first commercial was for FTD, which led to a variety of others. It was only a short matter of time before she began auditioning as an actress. In 1999 she was cast in an episode of *3rd Rock From the Sun*, the independent film *The Secret Life of Girls* and the TV movie *Sarah, Plain and Tall: Winter's End*. The following year saw her in an episode of *Touched By An Angel* and *Edward Fubbwupper Fibbed Big*, for which she provided her voice. An episode of *Friends* featured her in 2001, and in 2002 she provided her voice for *The Hunchback of Notre Dame II* while she co-starred as secret agent Gerti Giggles in the feature film *Spy Kids 2: Island of Lost Dreams*. She reprised the role of Gerti the following year in *Spy Kids 3D: Game Over*.

"Those films were, like five years ago, but they were a lot of fun," says Emily. "I loved *Spy Kids*, like any kid would. It has gadgets and flying — I was really into the movie and wanted to be in it. It was cool; I got to wear this belt with power stuff and lots of gadgets and lots of pockets that we use during the missions to fight other spy kids with."

Her biggest break has obviously been on *Hannah Montana*, with more people recognizing her from that than anything else she's done.

"Disney does a great job promoting us," she says. "Although I've done a lot of other work before this, people now scream, 'Lilly!' That's the only thing they know me for. But what most people don't realize is they think [the audition process is] automatic, like, 'Okay, you're Lilly!' But it isn't like that for anything. I think I probably auditioned three or four times. It was about a year and a half ago and I went in to read and at that time it was just a few people in the room. The last audition, Miley Cyrus was already cast and they wanted me to read with her. They want to see how you do on your own, how you work with the other actors, and eventually what you look like, what your qualities are, if you look the part. It just took a very long time. That's just how it works."

In drawing comparisons and contrasts between her and Lilly, Emily offers, "As weird as it is, I am kind of like Lilly. I am different from her, but I'm also very much like her. I'm really outgoing and I love hanging out with my friends and I'm just a

regular kid. I think I'm most like Lilly because I really like to do sports. She's a really sporty girl. She likes to get on her skateboard. And I think the way I'm sort of not like Lilly is she has, I have to say, the coolest clothes I have ever seen. Her clothes are so amazing, so I would love to have those kinds of clothes.

"I think Lilly's best quality is her ability to have fun all the time," she continues. "She's so energetic and she's always doing something crazy with Oliver or with Miley and they just have a ball together. And yes, she is a little bit crazy and she's not the brightest, but she has so much fun with both of them and she can just turn any situation into something positive. If it's bad, she can completely turn it around, and that's one thing that I think everybody

should try and do."

Success on *Hannah Montana* led to her starring in the TV movie adaptation of R.L. Stine's *The Haunting Hour: Don't Think About It*, which was released on DVD on September 4, 2007. "This is the first scary movie I've ever worked on," says Emily. "It was fun, because I got to be on the side of what scares you, instead of the one being scared."

Her character in the film, Cassie, is a Goth girl, a lifestyle she was genuinely unfamiliar with. "I personally don't know anyone like Cassie," she explains. "I approached this character by looking at the things that made her choose to be a Goth girl more than what she did as a Goth girl. That was really the complexity of the character and what made her tick. She was going through

have to have a social life," she points out. "I'm an eighth-grader and I'm battling boys and all this kind of stuff. And I think with Miley, she has more time. This is her world right now. Miley is music and acting and her social life as well, and for me, it's more school and acting and my social life."

While every Disney star seems to be recording a CD these days, Emily is not expecting to be one of them. "I sing in the shower," she told *Life Story* magazine. "I do the choir at school, but it's nothing like Miley. It's not as good as Miley, but I like to sing. My dad did a lot of musical theater. My mom did a lot of singing at weddings when she was younger. I've always just been out there, just singing — not professionally, but it has always been in my life."

Emily Osment admits that she probably wasn't as aware of the show's phenomenal following until it was put in her face. "I was doing a signing back in Pennsylvania, and there were seven thousand people waiting outside the mall! What is hard is being in the limelight constantly. It means you always have to do everything right. But having young girls look up to me is important. It's also about making the audience in general happy, and seeing their reactions. Whenever I meet someone or talk to someone on the phone, it's a great feeling knowing you've made their day or that they love the show. That's a great feeling. That's what this is all about — making people happy."

a rebellious stage like all teenagers do to some degree. The 'why' is more important than the 'what.'"

Probably the biggest challenge of Emily's career at the moment is dealing with the sometimes overwhelming popularity of *Hannah Montana*, although it doesn't seem to be something she's overly concerned with. "I'm going to a regular high school, which is a prep school, and I

mitchel musso

oliver oken

The final part of *Hannah Montana*'s primary triumvirate is the character of Oliver Oken, Miley's other best friend, who, like Lilly Truscott, is allowed to be in on the truth about Miley/Hannah. For the producers, there was no one but Mitchel Musso for the role.

Notes Peterman, "Mitchel came in and stole our hearts by doing a scene where he had to try to sneak in a second-floor window. He got down on his hands and knees and used our table as the building window and all we could see was a little part of his head and his eyes peering out. We knew he was the guy."

"The process of getting on was they first knew me from *Life is Ruff*," says Mitchel, "and then they called me in and said they wanted to see me for Oliver. So I went in for the first audition and I ended up coming back two or three times. On the fourth time I read with Emily and Miley for testing. After that, they called me in and I got the part. We shot the pilot and then seven or eight months later they said they wanted to make it into a series. I was just so excited, because I've shot a couple of pilots before, but none of them have ever been picked up. Just being on a TV show, you get to be the same person each week. The show is amazing. The script just writes itself now. We have a terrific cast."

Mitchel was born on July 9, 1991, in Garland, Texas, a suburb of Dallas, to Amuel Musso II and Katherine. His family also includes brothers Marc (who he co-starred with in *Secondhand Lions*) and Mason (the lead singer of the band Metro Station), as well as a dog named Stitch.

He was drawn to acting at a young age, with one of his earliest roles as wookiee Chewbacca in a children's remake of George Lucas's *Star Wars*. At about the same time he also started to audition for and was cast in a number of print ads and television commercials for such companies as McDonalds, Rand McNally, Sony PlayStation, and Hubba Bubba Bubble Gum. It wasn't long, however, before he started trying out for TV and film roles.

"It all started with my dad's best friend and he got my little brother into it," says Mitchel. "When my brother was into it, I thought that was so cool to be out there on TV. I got with the agency he was with, called Kim Dobson, which was a Texas agency. I got a Borden milk commercial and there was no looking back. I was like, 'Whoa!' I loved it. So I decided to give it a shot and now I'm here."

Most actors tell horror stories of how difficult it was for them to break in, how long it took, and how close they were to giving up the whole idea of acting. But that wasn't the case with Mitchel. "I was like ten or eleven when I went on my first audition, and I got the first thing I auditioned for. I didn't really think about getting rejected. Now it hits me how crazy everything works. But when I started out, I didn't think about it — it was just life. At the same time, my 'journey' has brought me a long way. I'm a little Texas kid. I'm a country boy. I decided to come out here [to L.A.] for pilot season after I did *Secondhand Lions* with Haley Joel Osment. And so my agent told me I should give it a shot. Ever since I came out here, it's been exciting and fast-paced. I love what I'm doing."

And he's been doing it since 2002 as a film actor, having appeared in 2002's *The Keyman* and *Am I Crushed?* He followed

with 2003's *Secondhand Lions* and 2004's *Oliver Beene*. A big year for him was 2005, during which he appeared on TV in *Hidden Howie*, *Avatar: The Last Airbender* (for which he provided his voice), *Stacked*, *Life is Ruff* and *Walker Texas Ranger: Trial By Fire*. Perhaps his most challenging role came in 2005 in the form of the animated *Monster House*, which utilized motion capture technology for its computer animation. The film dealt with a house that comes to life and terrorizes a group of teenagers.

"Actually, it was pretty intense," he reflects. "I had to wear a wetsuit and reflectors every day, and a cap that I had to glue on. We worked in a twenty-by-twenty room with about two hundred motion capture cameras around us. We worked for, I think, three months on it. It was in production for over five years. As an actor, it was definitely different. You couldn't use the exact same expressions and emotions and stuff that you can use in front of a live camera. There are things that are pulling your face down every once in a while, so it was tough. But I got used to it after the first couple of days."

Though playing Oliver on *Hannah Montana* keeps Mitchel busy, he's still found time to voice the character of Jeremy in Toon Disney's *Phineas and Ferb* and has branched out into music, recording a cover of "Lean on Me" that appeared on the *Snow Buddies* soundtrack and rocketed into the Disney Radio Top 10.

The success of *Hannah Montana* amazes Mitchel, particularly the response from the

Miley and Mitchel aren't the only siblings in their families that work together: her brother Trace and his brother Mason are both in the band Metro Station!

Mitchel's debut musical performance at Universal City Walk in July 2007

fans. "I knew it was a great show when we shot the pilot," he says, "that everyone on the show was nice . . . and that they were super-funny. But did I think it would be more successful than pretty much anything else on Disney? No, not at all. And I never knew how crazy things would be — that we would be posters and merchandise and traveling and that there would be crazy, ecstatic experiences . . . and that Miley would be touring. I don't think anyone knew how crazy it was going to get, or the fact that the girl fans would go so crazy with the magazines and the posters and 'be mine' and all that junk. It's crazy."

By the same token, he understands why it's so popular with people. "I think that everybody can totally relate to *Hannah Montana* in a way. You've got two friends who go through problems and you're there for them, there's trouble, gotta bail your friends out, you have fun with your friends. It's like real life, and I'm sure everyone can relate to it."

jason earles
JacksON STEWART

One of the primary approaches to storytelling on *Hannah Montana* is to tell "A" and "B" stories, with the "A" story usually involving Miley, Lilly and Oliver, and the "B" story centered on Robby and/or his son, Jackson. With the casting of actor Jason Earles, everyone involved felt they had a major find on their hands that really helped bring the cast to completion and allowed those "B" stories to soar.

"Jason represents the last and one of the most important parts of the show," says Peterman. "At the time, we thought this is the brother of a star and he's probably going to have issues with his sister being a star, so we

Jason and his wife Jennifer at the Emmys in September 2007

made the character have a ventriloquist dummy that he spoke through, because it allowed him to say things he couldn't normally say. Well, Jason was the only guy who made the dummy funny. Then we realized he's so funny and so strong, he doesn't need the dummy. So we got rid of the dummy and we kept Jason."

Although it's known that Jason Daniel Earles was born on April 26, what's not so clear is what year that was. The safe bet is that he's in his mid-to-late twenties. Born in San Diego, California, he became fascinated by the idea of acting at a very young age.

"I've been acting since early in elementary school," he recalls. "I started acting and doing plays in third grade. I was in *Hansel & Gretel* back then. I played Hansel. I always did plays in school from then on and tried to get into summer stuff. My parents were really supportive of me going into acting; they thought it was a good way for me to burn off my extra energy. In fact, they took time off work and came to school to watch. I was, like, 'Oh, this is a great way to get some attention.' From that point on, any time I could get into summer stock or touring Shakespeare in the Park or community theater or school plays, I would do as much of that stuff as I could. Then once I moved to California, that's when I started to try to act for film and TV. It was weird, because all of my experience had been stage, and TV is a totally different beast. Acting is acting, but the technical aspect is completely different. We have the benefit of a live audience on Fridays and we usually shoot about half or two-thirds of an episode in front of them. We pre-tape other scenes on Thursdays. And you can really tell there's a different energy on Fridays when we have the live audience laughing and going along on the ride with us."

Jason began appearing on television in 2003 on *MAD TV* and *The Shield*. The following year saw him on TV's *Still Standing* and the Nicolas Cage big screen adventure *National Treasure*, while 2006 had him guest starring on *Special Ed*, *One* and *One on One*, while he appeared in the made-for-DVD film *American Pie Presents: Band Camp*. But as is the case with his co-stars, it's his character on *Hannah Montana* that has already brought him more attention than all of his other roles put together.

He enjoys playing Jackson, despite the fact that the character is considerably younger than he is. "I think if you talk to any guy, you get to about sixteen and that's pretty much where you stop," he smiles. "You never feel older than that. Your interests stay the same. You like to work, you like to earn money, you like girls, electronics, cars, and it's all sort of the same. You learn when you have to be mature and when

you're allowed to let loose and be crazy. Since I'm on a kids' show, I'm allowed to let loose and be crazy. It keeps you young at heart."

As to the appeal of Jackson, he adds, "I think Jackson is really fun. He is a harmless troublemaker. As far as the show goes, if there is something kind of outrageous and funny that's going to happen to somebody it is usually Jackson. He gets himself into a lot of trouble over things like girls and cars and picking on his sister, but his intentions are never bad. Everything is always kind of light and playful. He really embraced the whole Southern California lifestyle where

he gets to go out and surf and chase these pretty girls and work on his car and enjoy that whole side. I think he could be better in school than he is, but his focus is kind of all over the place.

"In comparing us," Jason muses, "I think Jackson is a bit more outgoing than I am. I tend to be pretty calm in my regular life unless I get excited about something. I will say that I think if there's a party situation, Jackson and I would probably both be big attention-getters. We're definitely attention hogs that way. And we have a lot of the same sort of interests. But Jackson is a bit more nuts than I was and he gets into more

> **"You learn when you have to be mature and when you're allowed to let loose and be crazy. Since I'm on a kids' show, I'm allowed to let loose and be crazy."**

trouble than I did. I always try to avoid situations that cause trouble. I don't like being yelled at or being told that my parents are disappointed in me. That's the worst."

Jason admits that he did have a little bit of concern when he joined the show and learned that the father-daughter dynamic on the show would be the real thing; that he, in effect, would be part of a "family" in which his pretend father and sister were actually related. "I was really nervous when I first found out Billy Ray was going to be the dad," he says. "They've got all this history with each other and I am going to be the outsider. But they are classic southern hospitality. It took me all of two days to feel accepted."

Despite the success of the show and the fan acclaim its cast has gotten, Jason tries to keep his head on straight about the whole thing, very much aware that often the candle that burns twice as bright only burns half as long. "I will ride this wave as long as they will let me," he points out. "But I think always in the back of your mind you wonder, 'What's gonna happen after this?' I would personally like to use this show and the fact that they let me do so many off-the-wall, crazy, funny things to maybe transition into network sit-coms. I've got sort of a natural fit there to play the friend or the crazy office guy. So I think about that a little bit, but I think we're to be here for a little while."

SHANICA KNOWLES

AMBER ADDISON

Amber and Ashley are fellow students who seem to go out of their way to drive Miley and Lilly crazy or to show them up whenever possible. Shanica Knowles, who plays Amber, was born on November 17, 1990. She made her acting debut playing Vanessa in an episode of *Unfabulous*, joined *Hannah Montana* in its first season in 2006 and, in that same year, played Haley Sidery in the film *Brain Zapped*. This was followed with the character of Sierra in *Super Sweet 16: The Movie* and as Shauna Keaton in *Jump In!* She also performed on *The Next Big Thing*.

anna marie perez

ASHLEY DEWITT

Anna Marie was born on December 23, 1990. She got her first taste of "fame" when she appeared on a 2003 episode of *Star Search*, where she was a Junior Singer Finalist. In 2006 she served as the host of the *New Year Sing-Along Bowl-Athon*. In that same year she played the character Miracle Rose on the series *Cake* for 13 episodes and, of course, began playing Ashley on *Hannah Montana*. A guest appearance on the series *Just Jordan* followed in 2007 and in 2008 she provided her voice to the character of "Safety Patrol Member Hero" in an episode of the animated *Higglytown Heroes* and appeared in the Jonas Brothers Disney Channel movie *Camp Rock*.

moises arias

Rico

While many of the show's subplots, or "B" stories, have focused largely on Jackson and Robby, increasingly those "B" stories have also featured the character of Rico, son of the owner of the surf shop where Jackson works. Playing Rico is Moises Arias, who was born on April 12, 1994. His career officially began in a barely-on-the-radar appearance on an episode of *Everybody Hates Chris* in 2005. The next year was a busy one for him as he appeared in an episode of *The Suite Life of Zack & Cody* as Randall, in the feature film *Nacho Libre* as Juan Pablo, and on stage in *Water and Power* in the roles of Gibby, Gabby and Deer Dancer. It was in 2006 that he also made his first appearance on *Hannah Montana* as Rico. He played Mario in 2007's *The Perfect Game* and plays Andre in the Disney Channel 2008 movie *Dadnapped*.

51

CODY LINLEY
jake Ryan

Of all the people who have appeared on *Hannah Montana*, the one who has seemed to generate the most heat is Cody Linley as actor Jake Ryan, Miley Stewart's on-again/off-again boyfriend. He was born Cody Martin Linley on November 30, 1989, and raised in Texas. Basically one of the "veterans" of the cast, Cody made his debut in the 1998 TV movie *Still Holding On: The Legend of Cadillac Jack*. The year 2000 was a banner one for him as he had small roles in the films *My Dog Skip*, *Where the Heart Is* and *Miss Congeniality*. Between 2003 and 2006 he appeared in the feature films *When Zachary Beaver Came to Town* (as Cal), *Rebound* (playing Larry Burgess, Jr.), *Echoes of Innocence* (in the role of Christopher) and *Hoot* (a starring role of Mullet Fingers). In between he also guest starred on the Disney Channel's *That's So Raven* as Daryl. In 2007 he played Sean in *The Haunting Hour, Volume One: Don't Think About It*. As popular as Cody is as Jake, there's no word on whether or not he will be returning to *Hannah Montana*.

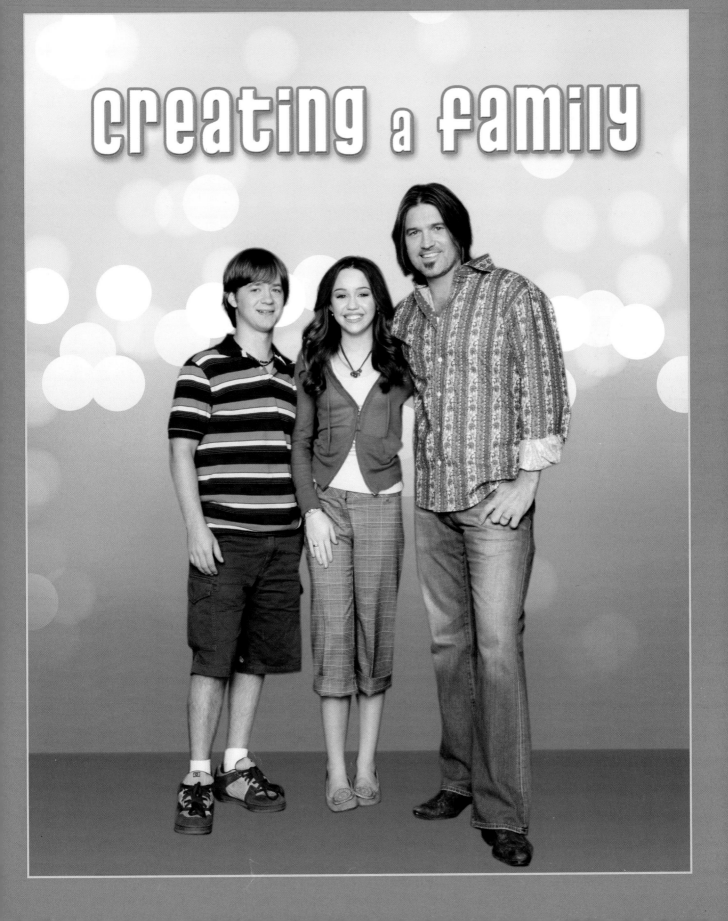

creating a family

With the show's cast in place, *Hannah Montana*'s producers took a step back, looked at the ensemble they'd gathered and believed that they had captured lightning in a bottle.

"We did our pilot, and Michael and I looked at each other and we said, 'We are going to be working on this until these kids are graduating college,'" reflects Peterman. "And so far, the reaction has been sensational. We have, I think, the highest-rated premier of any show in Disney Channel history. We're their highest live-action show. Kids are loving this show and I think parents are liking this show. We try to make it something the whole family can watch. We're having a ball, and it's getting to be more fun every week."

Part of the show's appeal may stem from the fact that the actors in front of the camera genuinely bonded with each other very quickly, forming something of a second family amongst themselves and growing protective of each other. For instance, when Billy Ray was asked about similarities between Robby's feelings over his daughter dating with the actor's real-life feelings, he offers, "Miley has always had a mind of her own. She's always been very strong. And, again, I've always just wanted her to live her life and be happy. At the same time, she's very smart. And 99.9 percent of the time I just trust that she's going to make good decisions, because that's what life is about, making good choices. I trust Miley. I truly trust her."

And here's where the second family element comes in, as Jason adds, "He also knows that I have his back. I'm really super, hyper-protective of her. Every time we have guy guest stars, I eyeball them if they get too close to her."

Laughs Miley, "Yeah, he comes up and I'll be, like, sitting here and I'll be flirtin' up a storm. And he'll walk up, 'So, Miley, those nachos, they're real good, huh?'"

"I just use the three-foot rule," Jason shrugs. "If there's any male guest cast members that are within three feet of her, I back them off a little."

Miley notes, "He steps in the middle and is, like, 'How you doing, dude?' And I'm, like, 'Yeah, Jason, you're real nice. We'll talk later.'"

Such moves on Jason's part definitely come from the heart. "Miley and I definitely love each other like brother and sister," he says. "I love her dad. I really feel like I've been embraced by the whole Cyrus family. They've got a really big family and they're all really, really cool. But we definitely have our moments where we bicker like brother and sister. I think any older brother that has a younger sister will probably say the same thing: in your heart you love them to death and it would take a minor act of God for you to say it out loud. You will mess with them all the time, but if anyone else messes with them, then you are the first one to defend them. If I hear somebody say anything negative about Miley, I'm the first to defend her. I'll jump in there and look out for her."

To get more of that sense of family, all one has to do is quiz the cast about life on the set. For instance, there's the issue of bloopers — those terrific mistakes the actors make while performing.

"There's a boyfriend episode and the guy and everybody on the show were in my room," recalls Miley, "and Emily decides to stick her foot out to see if I would fall. Not only do I fall, I do a Superman — I go in the air flat and my face hits the ground pretty hard. Then we had an indentation in my floor."

"But it was a friendly trip," Emily emphasizes. "It was, like, 'Hey, here's my foot, don't trip.'"

"And I just went flying," Miley laughs. "It was the scariest thing. Good thing the cameras weren't on, because Steve would use it. That and then with learning our lines we end up doing each other's lines."

Emily shakes her head, noting, "I get caught for this all the time — Miley will be doing a line and I'll be mouthing her words, and they'll be saying, 'Emily, stop mouthing her words!' I don't even know I'm doing it."

Miley explains that they rehearse so much that everyone's lines seem to blur. "I know her lines better than my lines," she says. "I hear hers, so it's kind of like in my head already. So memorizing them is pretty easy."

Jason details that they get a new script or revision of the script every day, including the day they actually shoot the episode. "Technically," he offers, "you have a day to learn your lines. You have the foundation for it on Monday. You maybe get sixty percent of it on Monday, then you get

to pick up another twenty percent on Tuesday, another twenty percent on Wednesday, then polish it off. It's within four days you have to have it cold."

"I also think that memorizing the lines is really easy," muses Mitchel, "because Steve and Michael and all the other writers totally capture all of our characters."

Enthuses Peterman, "They're so young that their brains suck it all up. I'm amazed at how quickly they get it, then at the end of the week it's flushed out and they're ready for the next week. They're unbelievable."

Emily chalks that up to a very good reason: "It's not like we're speaking a foreign language as these characters. We're playing

ourselves, basically. We're not saying things that would be out of the ordinary or hard to memorize. We're saying, 'Yes, I would say that.' There are a lot of things I'm saying where it's, like, 'Hey, I would totally say that to Miley.'"

Billy Ray would agree. "When I read the script of *Hannah Montana*, I said, 'You know what? This *is* Miley!'" he says. "Originally it was a little girl named Chloe. The writers kept hearing me call her Miley, and the day we shot the pilot they came and said, 'Everything Chloe is Miley.'"

What also holds the cast together is the lack of ego. They treat each other with respect and no one tries to overshadow the others.

"I've been doing this a long time," says Poryes, "and there's not one scene stealer here. They're an amazing group. Nothing makes any of them happier than the other one getting a big laugh. Without hesitation, there's not one bit of scene stealing amongst them."

Elaborates Jason, "If you see an opportunity for a good joke within a scene, we'll make suggestions to each other to try to make sure everybody in the cast gets the most out of the writing, as opposed to, 'Maybe if they don't catch that joke, then I'll look like I'm funnier in the scene.' There's no sentiment like that on the show. We're trying to make sure everybody gets the most mileage out of their material."

Peterman notes that one of the things that started happening was that other cast members would come to watch Jason perform his scenes. "Jason was the most accomplished actor when the show started," he says, "and Jason showed these kids how to dig in every scene for everything that was there and to bring extra stuff. And it's been wonderful. If you had been here for the first couple of episodes and compared it to the stuff we were doing just last week, they are just learning at an incredible rate. We thank Jason all the time because he was sort of conducting an early master class."

"We have a theme around the set," Jason says, "and it's 'Go big or go home.' Monday and Tuesday, especially in rehearsal, it's an opportunity to really play and try to make big choices. Sometimes it's silly and it doesn't work, but a lot of times you'll find your best stuff when you're hanging out there being big. Then if it's too much, these

"She's got that voice and she's not manufactured."

guys, they're your extra set of eyes and they'll make sure you don't do anything wrong. We just kind of adopted that philosophy, 'Go big or go home.'"

Peterman explains, "As originally written, *Hannah Montana* was not from any place in particular. But when Miley and Billy entered the equation, it gave us something that was pretty unique on TV. On so many American shows the characters are kind of undifferentiated America. It could be anywhere, but it's sort of on one of the coasts or maybe Chicago. But Miley and Billy are heartland. They're the part of America that is huge, but underrepresented on television, and that gave us a road into a unique view that has evolved as we listen to these people and we begin to shape the characters to who they are. We didn't put in some of the country stuff until Billy started throwing some of it in and Miley started throwing some of it in rehearsal, because this is how they talk. We would not have presumed to put them into that kind of a character, but when we saw this is really who they are, it became a part of the show."

As to why the audience connects with Miley so much, Poryes muses, "The audience feels they can touch her. They know her. They know her friends. She doesn't have an ego, and she's not all out of control and all of that. She's not just acting the role. The role is, in large part, a lot like she is. You can't lie to kids. They're seeing the genuineness on the screen. They're seeing that our cast really likes each other. Billy and Miley

love each other and have a wonderful relationship. You really see that.

"Miley has such a strong personality that we started to shift the character to accommodate who she was," he continues. "Originally the show was much more about introspection. Onstage, she was Hannah Montana and more in control. But as Miley, she didn't know how to deal with certain situations in her life."

Peterman emphasizes, "The reality is that Miley showed us you can't be a girl who gets on a stage in front of fifteen thousand people and owns it, and come offstage and be something else. Miley has inner strength that just continued to surprise us in the first year as she grew into this and dealt with the challenges of the show."

"And that made us discover that the character is the same," notes Poryes. "Miley behaves the same as Hannah, which is one of the big secrets."

Says Peterman, "It's that thing that differentiates us from every other kids show out there. We've got that life in it, and also Miley is the real deal. She's got that voice and she's not manufactured. Miley has the chops to play this character because she's become this character. Miley is a real girl who has become a rock star."

THIS IS THE LIFE
THE HANNAH PHENOMENON BEGINS

Right out of the gate, *Hannah Montana* proved itself to be a ratings juggernaut for the network, premiering with 5.4 million viewers and then averaging 3.5 million viewers a week in its first season. The show instantly connected with the show's desired tween audience, turning the show's cast — particularly Miley — into instant superstars.

"I think the reason the show works," says Miley, "is because everybody wants to follow their dreams. She gets to go for it, and people like to see that."

With her fame on the rise from the moment the show premiered, Miley herself admits that it's not always an easy balance to achieve between being a celebrity and living the life of a normal teenager. Ironically her real-life situation is mirroring that of her on-screen alter ego. In a way, it might be a relief for Miley Cyrus to be able to slip into a secret identity in the way that Hannah Montana does.

"Going in," she explains, "you know we'll be working and you have to be totally on and be really loud and running around and just being crazy. Then you have to go to school and sit there and focus. So it's kind of weird. All of our scripts are so amazing and we just want to be out here, performing. It's kind of hard to sit still. I guess the hardest part of all of this is keeping up the energy, because there's so many people to meet, so many things to do, and if we had a bad day, you don't want people to catch you on that day when you just don't feel like you could smile or look cute in a picture. So I think that's the hardest thing, keeping up your energy and making sure that you can really relate to all the people that you're going to meet.

"There are a lot of parts of fame," Miley continues. "Now that the show has taken off, you've got to keep everything fresh and think of new things to keep people interested in the show. But another, I think, great thing — and something that Emily would probably say, too — is a part of fame which people don't really see: you get to help people. You can really be an inspiration. We have this little thing called phone friends. We call people in the hospital with cancer and all kinds of diseases, and they get to ask us questions. It's really great to not only get to do what you love, but help other people reach their dreams, too."

Emily Osment agrees that there's really not a downside to fame, "except keeping everything balanced," she says. "We are kids. We need time to play and everything. But we are living the dream right now. This is what we've wanted to do all our lives. I'm finally doing it. It's a happy feeling. Especially doing things for people like phone friends and things like that. That's what it's all about, making people happy."

One amusing part of the show's fandom is the occasional blurring of the lines between the real stars and their on-screen alter egos, which reveals itself in the fan mail that Miley receives. "There's a picture some-one will send to Miley Cyrus of *Hannah Montana*, and a letter that says, 'Can you give this to Hannah Montana for me?'" she smiles. "So I was, like, 'Okay, I'll do that.' But, yes, Miley Cyrus gets a lot of mail, but Hannah Montana gets a lot of comments about her songs and stuff. So it's kind of equal in terms of the fan mail. Some of it's interesting. Some of it includes the lyrics of the songs, or they'll send me their favorite lines. Which is cool, because it lets you know what people are liking. Most of them are really cool to read."

One inevitable downside to their instant celebrity is the loss of privacy the actors have faced, as well as the fact that they can't really go out in public much without draw-ing attention to themselves. This is a fact of life that Miley merely takes in stride.

"Sometimes people are, like, 'Oh, I wish I could go out,' but all of my life I've just been working for this," she admits. "I've wanted this so much. Now that it's here, it's a part of this lifestyle. It's really not a bad thing, you know. It's really cool to get to see all the people that are out there supporting

you. It's so worth it to see all these young kids looking up to you. It's really awesome. So I can definitely take some personal expe-riences and bring them to Hannah

theme park] with my brother and a friend," Miley told the *Philadelphia Inquirer.* "The recognition was immediate. It was craziness — all the kids on every ride! I felt like I was going to hurl after one ride and the kids were, like, 'Hannah Montana is about to puke!' I used to go to the mall and people would be, like, 'You're on a show? What?' Now it's insane. Managers and everyone hate me. They're, like, 'Please get out of the store,' because it gets so insane. It's pretty crazy, how fast it all came. But it's cool to know people support you."

"I've always believed you should give them everything you've got," says Billy Ray of the fans. "I've seen her sign every autograph. She knows that the fans are what it's all about."

Emily muses, "I think we're all sort of experiencing some Hannah-isms in this. We're doing this right now three weeks out of the month, and we're sort of living what Hannah is living. She's being this pop star, then she has to live this normal life as Miley Stewart, and I think we're all doing that on hiatuses and things like that."

On the other hand, Jason says that he hasn't experienced such a seismic shift out in the real world. "I haven't really had very much recognition outside of this, which, personally, is kind of what I want," he says. "I enjoy coming here every day and hanging out with everyone and working, but the actual fame part of it is not what I'm really interested in. It's more about just doing the work. And Jackson on the show is the one

Montana. When there's scenes with me and Emily where Emily is starting to go to the shows and there are so many fans there that she gets to see, that's kind of how my friends are, too. Lilly, in the show, is thankful for her blessings that Hannah Montana had and so happy for her to get to live her dreams. That's how my friends are, too."

Which is not to say that the timing for public recognition is always . . . convenient. "I went to Universal [Studios Hollywood

that's kind of the outsider when it comes to show business. He gets to see it from the outside and kind of enjoys being on the fringe of it. I feel that's what my personal experience with the show has been so far, too."

"I haven't been noticed that much either," Mitchel points out. "But I've gone to a couple of things with Miley and she has just been *surrounded* by people. I think that's so cool. People have come up to me and they're like, 'Hey, you're Oliver.' You make them smile and they want your autograph and picture. I love it."

One exception both Jason and Emily noticed was when they appeared at a meet-and-greet held at Florida's Brookfield Zoo, where they had more problems with adults than with the kids.

"It would surprise you," Jason told the Florida *Sun-Times*. "It's the parents who are really, really aggressive. The kids are nice." To which Emily added, "Just trying to get through the airport to come here was crazy. One person spots you and then everybody comes over. And if you take one picture, you've gotta take everybody's."

Billy Ray does admit that he worries about everything that is happening to his daughter as her popularity seems to increase on a daily basis.

"I worry every day," he admitted to CMT.com. "Luckily we go back to our roots. We're a faith-based family. We've always tried to live for the light. I'm the last guy to cast a stone at anybody. I've made as many mistakes or more than any of those kids have made out there. But I tried to learn from my mistakes, so I'm hoping that Miley can look at my life and some of the other things around here and just learn so she doesn't have to make those mistakes. We pray every day that she's going to make good decisions. Then we pray every day that I'm gonna make a couple of good decisions, too. She's probably worried more about me than I am about her."

Faith remains extremely important to Miley, who offers, "It's the main thing. That's kind of why I'm here in Hollywood — to be like a light, a testimony to say God can take someone from Nashville and make me this, but it's His will that made this happen." In fact, it's Miley's faith that convinces her that she won't become the fodder for tabloids in the same way that people like Britney Spears and Lindsay Lohan have.

"We have a good family, and we have good close friends that would never let something like that happen," she says. "Before I came out here [to L.A.], my parents were, like, 'You know, there's no way that you can turn into any of that.' And also, just me as a person, I would never let that happen. I look at that and I see things are going on that are such bad things to put into girls' — guys', too, but mostly girls' — heads. I still go to church every Sunday with my family and really just want to learn, because I don't want to blend in with everyone. I just want to give a good image and a good message to girls, and guys, too. You know, you could look at other people, things that they're doing and you say to yourself, 'I don't want to make that mistake.' I definitely have people supporting me and helping me out when I'm not having such a good day or I'm feeling like things aren't going the best. Good friends and family help me along."

There's an old expression that what goes up, must come down, and one has to wonder whether or not there will reach a point where the tide of acclaim will turn against *Hannah Montana*; whether the media that loves the show so much now will start to criticize it. The cast doesn't seem that worried about the possibility.

"I've never dealt with any criticism," says Billy Ray. "You know, for every reaction, there's an equal and opposite reaction. If you do something that's really, really good or you do something that they really, really like, there's going to be somebody that really, really hates it. That's just the laws of life; that's just the way it is. So we just try to do what the fans of the show want us to do and be the best people we can be on this

earth while we're here. And hopefully do what makes us happy."

Adds Miley, "The truth is there's always going to be someone to criticize you for whatever, but you can't really take that personally. You make all your choices and you take it and you don't use it in a bad way and do what everyone wants. You know, take the criticism, make it happen and give them nothing to complain about. You know, I go to fan sites a ton. I love reading the chat boxes. It's so fun. You read that someone didn't dig this, but someone else loved it. You read all the opinions and some can be a little harsh. But you never can please everyone. That's one of the most important things that I've learned from my father: you can't make everyone happy. But on the other side of it, at my first record signing — it was at the Virgin Megastore in New York — there were so many kids there, screaming, 'I love you.' What makes it so special is to know that there really are kids who *do* love you. They really do have this love for you, and it's great to feel that from them."

"Criticism is inevitable," says Peterman. "And another wonderful thing about having somebody like Billy in the cast is Billy has been doing this long enough to experience the ups and downs of this business, and so he's kind of the one that everybody can look to for how do you survive for years in the business, because it isn't always great. And he has a wonderful perspective that, you know, is going to help Miley and is going to help all the rest of the cast, too."

SHE MIGHT EVEN BE A ROCK STAR

For the Walt Disney Company it was a formula that has literally worked for half a century: find a TV personality that connects with young viewers and groom them first for big-screen stardom and then, if they can carry a tune, a career in music. It worked with Annette Funicello from *The Mickey Mouse Club* half a century ago, just as it did more recently with Hilary Duff and Lindsay Lohan, who, respectively, made the leap from the *Lizzie McGuire* TV series and the movie remake of *Freaky Friday*, to the world of music.

In the case of someone like Hilary, the fact that she *could* sing was just a bonus. Miley Cyrus, on the other hand, left them no doubt of her talent: the Mouse House knew *exactly* what it was getting, though no one could have possibly suspected the impact Miley would ultimately have on the music industry.

"My dad thinks that I sang before I could talk," Miley shares. "I was always humming. I always loved music. Before I even started singing, I loved just listening to him play the guitar; or when we would pass someone in the mall playing violin, I would always tell them, 'I want to play, I want to play.' And I've always been writing. I got kind of an advantage, because I got to watch my dad write and I kind of got to pick it up instead of having to do class after class. I got to see how he put a song together.

"Usually I just have this amazing tug to go and write a song, and it's not anything that I would ever go and force," she continues. "It's just something personal. Whether it's writing books or poems, you never just sit down and say you have to write something. It has to come naturally, so it's not a step-by-step thing where I will just sit down and start writing and getting a tune in my head. Sometimes I will hear it and have something stick with me all day, and I will just go write about that or maybe something someone said. I will just take that and turn it into a song."

Back on October 16, 2006, Disney officially announced that Miley's debut album in the form of the *Hannah Montana* soundtrack would be reaching stores on October 24. The album featured eight songs from the show, performed by Miley as Hannah Montana: "The Best of Both Worlds," "Who Said," "Just Like You," "Pumpin' Up the Party," "If We Were a Movie," "I Got Nerve," "The Other Side of Me" and "This Is the Life." In addition to songs performed by Click Five, Jesse McCartney, Everlife and B5, the soundtrack album also featured a duet by Miley and dad Billy Ray, "I Learned From You."

On DVD June 26

Miley celebrates the release of the *Hannah Montana: Pop Star Profile* DVD with (from left to right) her brother Trace, mom Tish, sister Brandi and dad Billy Ray

When the disc was released, the audience was more than ready for it: it debuted at the #1 position on the *Billboard* 100, selling 281,000 copies in its first week — topping John Legend and My Chemical Romance. It stayed at the top in week 2, selling an additional 203,000 copies (and beating out Barry Manilow's debuting *The Greatest Songs of the Sixties*). It dropped to number 5 in week 3 (still selling 131,000 copies) and stayed in that position the following week and continued from there. Ultimately it would move over 3 million copies in the United States and an additional 3.5 million worldwide.

The Disney machine kicked into overdrive when a "holiday edition" of the album was released to iTunes on December 19, 2006. Besides all of the tracks from the original release, also included was "Rockin' Around the Christmas Tree," which Miley as Hannah performed at the Walt Disney World Christmas Day Parade on Christmas Day 2006.

But that *still* wasn't it, as a two-disc

Special Edition was issued on March 30, 2007. This one, in a holographic silver box, included the contents of the original disc, "Nobody's Perfect" from the season 2 soundtrack, four autographed photos of Miley Cyrus, a PIN for a "This Is the Life" ringtone, and a DVD featuring the "Nobody's Perfect" music video, a thirty-minute *Hannah Montana: Backstage Secrets* and a trailer for the DVD *Hannah Montana: Pop Star Profile*.

Whereas Disney felt Miley needed a little bit of help on the first *Hannah Montana* soundtrack (hence the inclusion of other artists), there were no such necessities on the follow-up, *Hannah Montana 2/Meet Miley Cyrus*. In fact, for the first time Miley was being allowed to "reveal" herself apart from her on-screen alter-ego as each disc in the two-disc collection would feature ten tracks, the first performed by Hannah and the second by Miley.

Early on in the process, Miley offered, "I get on with my own thing [on the disc] — a little country and then pop and rock and some bluegrass. I play guitar. I've recorded some demos with my friends. I'm excited about it, because everybody knows Miley Stewart and everybody knows Hannah Montana. But people don't know Miley Cyrus, the person underneath."

Later she added, "The songs on the show are cool, they're fun, they're young, but they're written for the character. I'm excited and anxious to see what people think of my songs as well. They'll be meeting me in those songs and hearing more personal stories. I'm kind of nervous to put them out, because some are so personal. They're real-life stories in which people can see me personally and see I'm just a normal girl. I think it's good to just go all the way and really let them see who you are. If I'm in this for the long run, then I don't want to fake it. I want people to see the real me. They can see enough of me acting on TV."

Released on June 27, 2007, *Hannah Montana 2* featured songs from the second season of the hit show while *Meet Miley Cyrus* showcased Miley's songwriting talents on eight of the ten tracks. In a Disney press release, Cyrus said, "I'm so excited for fans to hear my solo material! The music is introducing you to Miley Cyrus, the girl underneath the wig. The songs are personal and will give fans a chance to understand and relate to me. Listening to the lyrics will also show why I love doing what I do — singing, acting and dancing."

Like its predecessor, *Hannah Montana 2/Meet Miley Cyrus* debuted at the top of the *Billboard* charts (beating Kelly Clarkson's new disc), blowing past its predecessor's debut by selling 326,000 copies in its first week and remaining in the top five for its first ten weeks of release. Also like its predecessor, it was only the first release of the disc: *Hannah Montana 2: Rock Star Edition* was released on December 5, 2007 (conveniently just in time for the holidays). Focusing only on the *Hannah Montana* part of the original CD release, disc one features the bonus tracks of an acoustic version of "One in a Million" and the song "We Got the Party," which features the Jonas Brothers. Disc two is a "music video" DVD featuring "Life's What You Make It," "Old Blue Jeans," "One in a Million," "Make Some Noise," "True Friend," "Nobody's Perfect" and "Bigger Than Us."

"If I'm in this for the long run, then I don't want to fake it. I want people to see the real me. They can see enough of me acting on TV."

Finally, on January 29, 2008, Disney released *Hannah Montana 2: Non-Stop Dance Party*, which, again, focuses solely on the Hannah tracks from *Hannah Montana 2*, featuring remixes of "We Got the Party," "Nobody's Perfect," "Make Some Noise," "Rock Star," "Old Blue Jeans," "Life's What You Make It," "One in a Million," "Bigger Than Us," "You & Me Together," "True Friend," and "Hannah Montana Mega ReMix."

For Miley, finishing up the release and promotion of *Hannah Montana 2/Meet Miley Cyrus* was a relief, and it was a joy for her to return to the production of the series. "Everything is slowing down," she said shortly after the disc's release. "Just doing the show is such a break for me. I was on tour with The Cheetah Girls, went to London and Paris, was getting the word out about the new *Hannah* CD and Miley CD — I'm now working for two people. And writing. I write all the time. Miley Cyrus wrote every song on that CD. I write in my sleep. I don't know how, but I'll work on a song, go to sleep and it's finished when I wake up."

During the PR work she did, the one question she was faced with over and over again was whether she preferred music or acting over the other. "Music is easier for me, because I've been writing for a long time and I've been singing and going on tour with my dad," she said. "Acting was harder at the beginning. But once you finish

an episode, you never have to think about those lines ever again — they are out of your mind. That's the easy part about it.

"I would be writing songs when I was younger," she continued, "and try to put silly things together about me and my dad, and my name and all these silly things that we would write. And I would love people to hear what I had written. So I think it's kind of like an instant thing when you sit down and you work really, really hard, and then you kind of immediately get to see what people's reactions are, so if there's a couple of changes you need to make, you can do it. I guess songwriting got easier as I learned the process of it."

making some noise

Hannah and Miley live in concert

"They came. They screamed. And just when you thought they couldn't possibly scream anymore, they screamed even louder."

Thus began *The Dallas Morning News* review of a Miley Cyrus as Hannah Montana concert, which appeared in the paper on October 6, 2006. And for the most part, it seems to sum up any of the performances she's given since. The crowds have gotten larger, and the response even more powerful and excited.

Amazingly, that excitement is something that Miley herself shares. "There's nothing more fun than being out on stage and getting the vibe from the crowd," she enthuses. "I remember when I first started going to my dad's concerts. I started watching to see the crowd just go wild for the music and see the reactions. Then I really knew that's what I wanted to do, because I love being entertained. I love having an audience."

But does she ever get nervous in front of an audience? "The weird thing is, and everybody doesn't understand this, I actually get less nervous when it's a huge crowd. When there's that many people, you can't really see what's going on. But when it's a small crowd, you can see every little face. If I look down and see somebody who, you know, is waiting for the next performer, I get so embarrassed and so shy. So I like it better when it's a big crowd."

When Miley started, the crowds weren't as big as they are now and they were more controlled, particularly because those concert performances were being staged and filmed for episodes of *Hannah Montana*. But then Miley got the opportunity to start performing in public for real (always in her Hannah guise) on morning news shows, events like the Macy's Thanksgiving Day Parade, and as an opening act for groups like The Cheetah Girls. Eventually, though, she got the opportunity to headline her

own tour and was even allowed to perform concerts as herself "with" Hannah, with one opening for the other.

When Disney announced Miley's Best of Both Worlds tour in August 2006, it was a unique concept in that she would open the concert as Hannah Montana and sing songs from the show's two soundtrack albums. And then, after an intermission, she would appear as Miley Cyrus and perform her own music. The sixty-nine-date tour started on October 18, 2007, in St. Louis and concluded in Miami on January 31, 2008. One dollar from each ticket sold was donated by Miley to the City of Hope, a cancer research and treatment hospital in Duarte, California.

So what is a Miley/Hannah concert like? The *Oregonian* writes, "By the end of Cyrus's ninety-minute, seventeen-song set, I was captivated by the *Hannah Montana* experience and figured out why she's so enormously appealing to girls between eight and twelve. For starters, there's the clothes. Cyrus had seven costume changes, an array of sequined tops, shiny boots and glittering jeans that were more Technicolor than a Disney cartoon. And everything was covered in cascades of glitter. . . . And this girl can move and sing. Whether she was being herself or her secret alter-ego Hannah, Cyrus and her ten back-up dancers and singers covered every inch of the stage and its catwalk . . . The whole 'Hannah'/Miley dual identity of both the TV series and arena show is irresistible, too. As 'Hannah,' she's an international sensation. But she can retreat to being Miley, a regular teen unencumbered by the pitfalls that typically come with stardom."

Offers *The Atlanta Journal-Constitution*, "The production values were Disney-level impressive, with a tri-level stage, huge video screens, confetti and eight back-up dancers, who dressed up like teens but looked far beyond high school age. Cyrus, as her alter ego Hannah Montana, dressed in spangly, bright dresses and sang upbeat pop tunes about 'Life's What You Make It' and I'm-just-a-regular-gal cuts such as 'Just Like You'

and 'Nobody's Perfect.' The second half of the concert featured Cyrus's 'normal' brunette self. She opened as a rocker chick, with some leather and chains thrown in, but this is Disney edgy so it wasn't anything the parents would find alarming. She eventually donned a dress for a Latin-inspired 'Let's Dance,' then wore a Catholic schoolgirl uniform for the *Hannah Montana* theme song, 'Best of Both Worlds.'"

"The entire show operated at a frenzied fever pitch," adds *The Los Angeles Times*, "but its David Cronenberg–like climax came right before the encore, when the regular girl sang a duet with her famous alter-ego, who'd disappeared from the stage but now reappeared on the screen of a giant video monitor."

Reviews www.guidelive.com, "If her fans were indeed too quiet, it was only because some of them were in abject shock.

Miley closes the show with "Ready, Set, Don't Go," a duet with her dad along with sister Brandi on guitar

Here was the girl who has invaded their TVs, radios, books, backpacks and inner psyches standing in front of them, in real life. But that trance was quickly broken by their urge to jump up and down and join the masses in shrieking. When the star said she had only one rule — 'I never want to look out there and see anyone sitting down!' — they took the command seriously. And she was watching; after almost every song, the fourteen-year-old would pause for a long water break and simply smile into the crowd, as if she wanted to take it all in. As she should."

In every move that she has made and through each stage of her young career, Miley Cyrus has absolutely proven herself to be a genuine superstar, and if what we've seen so far continues, that star is going to continue to soar higher and higher.

if THEY WERE a movie

HANNAH MONTANA ON THE BIG SCREEN

It would seem that 2008 is the year that *Hannah Montana* makes the leap to the big screen.

First off, there was the 3D concert film that opened in theaters on February 1, which brought her Best of Both Worlds tour to the big screen. Of that film event, Walt Disney Studios' Dick Cook offered, "Miley is one of the most exciting and talented performers of her generation, and watching her on the concert stage is a gen-

uine thrill. As soon as she committed to the Best of Both Worlds tour last winter, we wanted to find some special way to let all of her fans share the excitement and fun of this live event, and filming the concert in 3D seemed like an ideal way to do that."

The concert tour was directed and choreographed by Kenny Ortega, who had done the same for the *High School Musical* and Cheetah Girls movies and tours, and his strong creative force is felt throughout the concert performance. While most of the film is essentially the concert, it's the backstage sequences that are most revealing — showing just how hard Miley works in juggling the TV series, the music rehearsals, school and her personal life. Her father Billy Ray introduces her to the band members he's worked with, briefly rehearses a duet with Miley (which, unfortunately, we don't get to see in concert), and learns Miley's song, "I Miss You." Mom Tish is also very present, taking on the role of "lead dresser," and coaching Miley in one instance where she was uncomfortable with a lift dance move. The Jonas Brothers are a welcome bridge between the Hannah Montana and Miley Cyrus parts of the concert, and their off-stage camaraderie with Miley is evident. The digital 3D enhances the viewing experience, especially showing the "depth" of the band, back-up singers and dancers. (There's one take of the drummer throwing a drumstick in the air that works so well in 3D.) The marketing of *Best of Both Worlds* was also innovative for

Disney. Originally it was to only play for one week (February 1–7), and in a limited number of cinemas with the Disney website linking to the box-office systems of each theater. As a result, the first week sold out well in advance, the cinemas added additional show times, and the film captured the #1 box-office spot! The movie run was extended "by popular demand," first for one more week, and then weeks continued to be added as demand remained strong. On hitting #1 at the box office, Miley told Ryan Seacrest in a radio interview that she was "super stoked" and thankful for everyone's hard work on the film.

As excited as fans were with that film, it was nothing compared to the anticipation they're feeling regarding *Hannah Montana: The Movie*, which Disney says will reach theaters in 2008 despite the 2007–08 Writers Guild of America strike.

"I'll probably get in trouble for saying this," Billy Ray Cyrus told *The Tennessean*, "but they're looking at the state of Tennessee to do the feature for *Hannah Montana*. They're talking about coming to Nashville and bringing in some of our friends and people that have been on the show and some other people around town to come out and be a part of the feature. If that happens, I'm going to love it, 'cause I'll get to come here and hang out for a little while."

Actually it won't be all fun and games for Billy Ray,

based on what Miley revealed at the Los Angeles premiere of *Harry Potter and the Order of the Phoenix*: "My dad is the producer, which I'm really excited about. He's never done anything like this before, but my dad is ready to take on new challenges. Now we're figuring out ideas for the movie."

In an interview with MTV, Billy Ray revealed, "There will be a lot of similarities to the show and the fact that Miley is so real, her music is real, we'll keep a lot of that realism. But I think we'll go a little further with the comedy. And it's going to be on the big screen, so we'll try to make everything look bigger."

Added Miley, "The best idea [for the story] is that I miss home. So if we could maybe film in Nashville and everyone could see our house and where we live, that we have a farm, that would be really exciting."

At this point, the assumption is that unlike the situation with *Lizzie McGuire*, which was over by the time the movie version reached theatres, *Hannah Montana* on the Disney Channel will still be continuing with new episodes, thus the legend of Hannah Montana will go on.

On her horse, Miley with her family at their Nashville home in 1996

LiFe's WHaT SHe Made iT

THe miLey CyRUS NeWS DiaRy

A MONTH-BY-MONTH LOOK AT MILEY'S RISE TO SUPERSTARDOM

NOVEMBER 2003

♥ The *Daily Times* of Salisbury, Maryland, makes mention of the fact that Billy Ray Cyrus's TV series *Doc* will be airing, and that it will feature "Destiny Hope (Miley) Cyrus" reprising her role of Kiley.

AUGUST 2005

✿ According to the trade publication *Daily Variety*, the Disney Channel has given the greenlight for twenty episodes of *Hannah Montana*, which is described as a "comedy revolving around a pint-sized pop star who has an alternate identity in order to continue living life as a 'normal kid.'" The article also mentions that *Hannah* was one of two pilots the network was considering, the other being *Stevie Sanchez*, a *Lizzie McGuire* spin-off.

FEBRUARY 2006

♥ The first-ever World's Fair For Kids, described as the country's "largest interactive family event," was announced for an April 15–23 run in Orlando, Florida, at the Orange County Convention Center. According to the announcement, the fair would serve as the home base of eighteen pavilions, six interactive "worlds," three stages, a competition zone, a sports stadium, the Kids World Mall, and the Kids World Kafe. A number of singers were announced for the event,

among them Miley Cyrus in what would be one of the few times until more recently that she performed as herself rather than as Hannah Montana.

MARCH 2006

❀ In an interview that appeared in the *Chicago Tribune*, Miley was asked a number of questions. Among them was what audiences could expect from *Hannah Montana*. "After the pilot," she replied, "everyone will be able to understand what Miley and Hannah are going through. Mostly, it's going to show Hannah being a regular girl, and show that even if you're a star, you still have to go through a lot of what other girls

go through. So you'll see boyfriends and you'll see friends fighting. You'll also get Hannah doing what she loves to do." She was also asked whether or not she was ready for her real life to take on Hannah-like qualities in terms of public recognition. "I'm getting there," she said. "From the commercials and concerts that are on, I'm starting to get recognized a little. The other day at Subway some little girl recognized me. That was really fun. I said, 'I love this!' and everyone said, 'After a while you're not going to.' But I find it very cool."

★ The series premiere of *Hannah Montana* far surpassed anyone's biggest guess in terms of ratings, pulling in over 5.4 million viewers. Offered Disney's Gary Marsh, "This is an unbelievable response — beyond our wildest expectations. *Hannah Montana* has broken out like no other Disney Channel series ever."

APRIL 2006

♥ Walt Disney Records announced the forthcoming release of the *Disneymania 4* CD (described as a showcase of 15 tracks from today's biggest teen and tween stars) and *Disney's Karaoke Series: Disneymania Volume 2*. Naturally (otherwise why would we be mentioning it here?) Miley Cyrus is represented, in this case with "Zip-A-Dee-Doo-Dah" from *Song of the South*, which was recorded for *Disneymania 4*.

❀ *People* magazine interviewed both Miley and Billy Ray Cyrus, the resulting piece nicely demonstrating the interplay between the two of them. For instance:

> Miley: I get to do crazy stuff I wouldn't normally get away with, like pour Chinese food all over him [her dad]. And when you got that load of cake in the face!
>
> Billy Ray: I see a theme.
>
> Miley: I talk to the writers and make sure he gets hit with something at least twice a week.

★ While speaking to *The Biloxi Sun Herald* early in the show's run, she described the series as follows: "It's about a rock star who just wants to be with her friends and family and be a normal girl and she tries to go in disguise and not show everyone she's a rock star, because she's supposed to be normal. So she goes in disguise and puts on wigs and tons of makeup. At the end she has her friends, but she also has her secret life of being a rock star." And of having to switch personas each episode, she added, "It gets difficult sometimes, because I'll be in the same place but being two people, so I'll have to run back and forth and take the wig off and be two different people at the same time. They both have different attitudes, so you've got to change quickly."

❀ Miley announced that music was about to become a very important part of her life, and that she would be singing on a soundtrack album to *Hannah Montana*, which was scheduled for a summer 2006 release. "I just signed with Hollywood Records," she enthused, "so singing is going to take a big part of the future. I'm singing on every song [on the album] and I'll also be doing a little bit of touring."

★ Speaking with *Newsday*, Miley was asked to draw a comparison between Hannah Montana and herself. "I'm like Hannah because we value the same things," said Miley. "The show's all about being with your family and friends. But Hannah's got better style than me. Her clothes are amazing!"

MAY 2006

♥ With the announcement of the 40th Annual Country Music Awards came the news that Miley and Billy Ray Cyrus would serve as presenters.

JUNE 2006

⭐ Miley appeared on the June 20 edition of *Live With Regis and Kelly* to promote the upcoming soundtrack to *Hannah Montana*.

JULY 2006

⭐ For Miley fans, Radio Disney had a great announcement: "In celebration of its tenth birthday, Radio Disney will present a live webcast of its star-studded, sold-out concert, the Radio Disney Totally 10 Birthday Concert on Saturday, July 22, 2006, at 7 p.m. (PST)." Fans could log on to RadioDisney.com to attend the virtual concert. Billed as the biggest concert event in Radio Disney history, the Radio Disney Totally 10 Birthday Concert was to feature hot artists, including Jesse McCartney, Bowling For Soup, The Cheetah Girls, Aly & AJ, Everlife and Miley Cyrus as Hannah Montana.

✿ The *San Jose Mercury News* announced a September 19 concert by The Cheetah Girls, featuring Miley Cyrus as Hannah Montana as an opening performer. The show was to take place at the HP Pavillion at San Jose. This was to be the first in a forty-city concert tour.

AUGUST 2006

♥ American Express, Blockbuster, Inc., and Disney announced that they were partnering with Boys & Girls Clubs of America to launch Boys & Girls Clubs Day For Kids, a major new family event that, annually, will serve to highlight the value of meaningful time between caring adults and children. The first such event would be scheduled for September 16, with Miley and Billy Ray Cyrus serving as spokespersons. Offered Billy Ray, "Miley and I have a great relationship. I think it's important as parents and neighbors that we spend quality time with children and to encourage others in our communities to do the same." Added Miley,

Miley with The Cheetah Girls and *Suite Life*'s Brenda Song (second from left)

"My dad and I talk all the time about the important stuff in my life. He and my mom know how much I appreciate them and our relationship is good because we spend time together. I am happy to be a part of this day to help other kids feel the same way."

SEPTEMBER 2006

❀ Given the international success of *High School Musical*, which was translated for local audiences in, among others, Italy, Japan and Spain, Disney expressed a desire to see *Hannah Montana* do the same. Noted Disney Channel Worldwide President Rich Ross, "Miley Cyrus is the most honest, funny and talented actress we may ever have worked with. I think she will be the toast of Asia before you know it."

★ In an interview with the *Biloxi Sun Herald*, The Cheetah Girls discussed their tour and their opening acts, including, of course, Miley Cyrus. "We are so excited [about Miley]," said Sabrina Bryan. "We had a chance to really get to know Miley when we were doing some Disney Channel promotions, and she is so sweet. We're already trying to think of what we're going to get her as a wrap gift on tour. We're going to sing a remake of 'Girls Just Wanna Have Fun' with Miley and Vanessa [Anne

Hudgens]. We've never had anyone on stage with us before, so it's going to be exciting."

OCTOBER 2006

♥ While speaking to the *Atlanta Journal-Constitution*, Miley was asked about her friendship with *High School Musical* and *Suite Life of Zack & Cody* star Ashley Tisdale and what they do when they hang out, to which Miley replied, "Shopping! The other day we went shopping by her house and we got in a store and a big bunch of kids came in, and we were trapped. Then it doesn't help that here comes Vanessa from *High School Musical* into the store, too. They finally had to close the store down!"

🌸 The Omaha *World-Herald* reviewed the DVD release *Hannah Montana, Vol. 1: Living the Rock Star Life*, noting, "From the Disney Channel, the series has the charm of *Lizzie McGuire*, and Cyrus is a charismatic young performer. Extras on the DVD include an unaired episode, Miley Cyrus's audition tape, a Hannah Montana music video and other extras."

★ Miley and Billy Ray sang the national anthem at Game 4 of the Cardinals vs. Tigers World Series.

♥ Disney was amazed at the popularity of Hannah Montana Halloween costumes. "There's been such a huge request, that we're letting kids know how they put one together themselves," explained Disney Vice President Adam Sanderson. "The signature item is that honey blonde wig. That and the right pair of sunglasses, a pair that say rock star. From there, you need jeans, boots and a rhinestone jacket or scarf. And you've got to have a pen to sign autographs, because you're a rock star, after all."

NOVEMBER 2006

♥ The soundtrack to *Hannah Montana* debuted at #1 on the *Billboard* Top 200 Chart, scanning over 281,000 units for the week ending October 29. This marked the first-ever TV soundtrack to enter that particular chart at #1. Additionally, the soundtrack earned the top position on both the *Billboard* Children's Chart and the *Billboard* Soundtrack Chart, and actually shipped platinum (1,000,000 units).

❀ While covering the Country Music Awards, the *Star Tribune* of Minneapolis, Minnesota, under the category of "Star in the Making Award," observed of the interplay between presenters Miley and Billy Ray, "It may have been scripted, but they didn't act like they were reading cue cards. Miley Cyrus told Billy Ray to take off his sunglasses, and he snapped, 'I don't tell you what to wear.' And she retorted, 'That's right. Remember the mullet.'"

★ The *New York Times* announced its sixth annual Arts & Leisure Weekend to be held January 5–7, 2007, with cultural institutions participating throughout the United States and Europe. The Weekend is the *Times'* annual signature event, a national and international celebration of art and culture. It includes interviews by *Times* journalists with celebrated artists, and special offers at cultural institutions around the world. Among those people scheduled to participate were Miley and Billy Ray.

♥ Miley performed as Hannah Montana in the Macy's Thanksgiving Day Parade.

DECEMBER 2006

★ Miley appeared on *VH1 Big in '06 Awards*, which paid homage to the biggest stars, the biggest moments and the biggest crazes of the year.

offered the *New Year Sing-Along Bowl-Athon*, which ran from 7:30 p.m. to 12:30 a.m. The program featured lip-synched performances of many of the songs from Disney's giant hits *High School Musical* and *The Cheetah Girls 2*. Having a hand in the fun were Miley, *The Suite Life of Zack & Cody*'s Dylan and Cole Sprouse and Brenda Song, *High School Musical*'s Ashley Tisdale and Corbin Bleu, and *Cory in the House*'s Kyle Massey.

JANUARY 2007

♥ *Billboard* took a look at Disney's growing music fortunes, saying of *Hannah Montana*, "When trying to quantify the heat surrounding [the show], try this one on for size: The soundtrack to the show has sold more than 1.9 million units since its release last November. It has also placed a whopping eight singles on the *Billboard* Hot 100. Now Cyrus is scheduled to release a solo album in June via Hollywood Records . . . The album will feature a mix of Cyrus originals as well as tracks from season two of *Hannah Montana*. And in the *pièce de resistance*, an accompanying tour is being discussed in which Cyrus will serve as the opening act for, that's right, herself."

❀ Miley was among the artists announced for the 2007 Livestock Show and Rodeo in Houston, Texas, to be held in March.

★ When *Sweet 16* magazine announced their list of the 16 Sweetest Stars 16 and Under, naturally Miley was on it.

❀ Of the *Hannah Montana* soundtrack, the Associated Press reported, "[The disc] has reliably sold over 100,000 copies a week, racking up a total of 1.6 million sold in two months . . . The 13-song *Hannah* disc has remained in the top 10 of the *Billboard* 200 album chart for all eight weeks it has been in release. During that same period, many new titles by stars, even those that debuted high on the chart, have plummeted quickly."

★ Miley was among the celebrities who participated in the ABC-TV special *Walt Disney World Christmas Day Parade.*

♥ On New Year's Eve, the Disney Channel

FEBRUARY 2007

⭐ Nickelodeon announced the 20th Annual Kids' Choice Awards, for which it was revealed that Miley had been nominated in the category Favorite Television Actress.

MARCH 2007

♣ Miley was announced as one of the new members to the American Red Cross National Celebrity Cabinet for 2007, which promotes "awareness of Red Cross services in a variety of ways, such as taping public service announcements; donating their time, money and blood; feeding victims of disaster; and generally lending a hand or a hug to those in need."

⭐ When Disney announced the launch of D*Concert: Disney Channel Concert Series, Miley (actually Hannah Montana) was among those featured, the others being The Cheetah Girls and the cast of *High School Musical.*

♥ Disney went public with plans to turn *Hannah Montana* into a global sensation. Writes journalist Anne Becker, "Disney will unleash an international marketing blitz, sending the show's teenage star to Europe to roll out a DVD, honor a theme park in

Paris and rock a concert in London in what will be an accelerated strategy to build on the year-old show's top ratings. Hannah's Miley Cyrus will launch the series' DVD compilation in Europe with appearances at the fifteenth anniversary of Disneyland Paris, a performance in London that will run later as a TV special and PR stunts throughout the continent."

APRIL 2007

♥ According to Disney, plans were afoot to remake 1987's *Adventures in Babysitting* (which had marked the directorial debut of Chris Columbus, whose subsequent credits include the first two *Home Alone* and *Harry Potter* films), with Miley Cyrus in the lead role and *That's So Raven*'s Raven-Symone in a supporting role. The original had starred Elisabeth Shue as a babysitter who gets involved in a wacky adventure with the kids she's babysitting for. The new film, to be titled *Further Adventures in Babysitting*, was announced to be written by Tiffany Paulsen, whose previous credits include *Fast Girls* and *Nancy Drew*.

✿ Mileymania struck London throughout April. Reports *The Mirror*, "Last week tweens went crazy when they heard she was coming to the U.K. for a one-off gig, with more than 100,000 children jamming switchboards. And her self-titled CD is poised to go platinum . . . Hannah mania has arrived. 'Our switchboard had 80,000 calls in just one day,' says Disney's London spokesman. 'Hannah Montana is like the

teenage equivalent of Elvis.' A screaming throng of 500 competition winners watched her perform at London's Koko Club. Hundreds queued for hours at HMV in Oxford Street waiting from 5 a.m. for their hero to sign copies of her DVD, *Behind the Spotlight*. Miley says, 'I love London. I love all the cool buildings. The biggest thing — I feel like such a geek — is all the taxis and the way that people drive on the opposite side. Even the little things you guys don't think about I think are totally awesome."

♥ *Disneymania 5*, the latest in the series of CDs featuring classic Disney songs sung by current stars, debuted at #14 on the *Billboard* Top 200 chart. Artists on this collection included Miley singing "Part of Your World," from *The Little Mermaid*, the Jonas Brothers, The Cheetah Girls, Jordan Pruitt, Vanessa Anne Hudgens and Corbin Bleu.

★ Miley sang the national anthem at the White House the day after Easter as a part of the annual White House Easter Egg Roll. Following Miley's performance, First Lady Laura Bush expressed, "I want to acknowledge the members of Congress and the members of the President's Cabinet that are here. And I especially want to thank Miley Cyrus for singing the national anthem. Wasn't she terrific?"

♥ According to Disney, one of Miley's British concerts would debut on the Disney Channel UK on May 7, and then be broadcast on Disney outlets across Europe, all in a means of spreading the word about Miley and Hannah Montana.

Miley beams at her audience after performing the national anthem at the White House.

MAY 2007

✿ ABC's *Good Morning America* went public with their summer concert schedule, noting that Miley would be performing as Hannah Montana on June 22.

♥ Thanks to the Children's Dream Fund, eight-year-old Samantha Lee, who is suffering from cancer, had a dream come true when she was flown from Florida to Los Angeles to the set of *Hannah Montana*, where she was given a behind-the-scenes tour, was able to watch a rehearsal and spoke to Miley Cyrus. "I felt really, really surprised," Samantha told *The Tampa Tribune*, "because [Miley's] a pop star, and she usually doesn't have much time."

JUNE 2007

★ Miley attended the 2007 Licensing Show to participate in the announcement of further extensions in the *Hannah Montana* brand, including new clothing and youth electronics, some of which would be demonstrated at the licensing show itself.

✿ Walt Disney Records and Amazon.com teamed up for an exclusive, live interactive interview with Miley Cyrus that was webcast on Amazon.com. It was the second such event for Amazon, which had previously featured director Alfonso Cuaron on *Children of Men*. Peter Fancy, Vice President of Music and Movies at Amazon.com, enthused, "We are excited to offer our customers a rare

opportunity to watch and interact directly with one of today's most popular teen role models, Miley Cyrus." Added Walt Disney Records Vice President of Sales Susan Van Hosen, "By partnering with Amazon.com on this innovative event, we are offering Miley Cyrus and Hannah Montana fans around the world an unprecedented opportunity to interact directly with their favorite star."

♥ Disney launched a *Hannah Montana* clothing line designed to appeal to fans of the show. "Among the offerings, modeled by Hannahs even younger than 14-year-old Miley," reported The Associated Press, "a denim jumper with rhinestones, slim-cut Bermuda shorts, cargo-pocket capris with swaths of silver, a sundress topped with a denim vest and a sheer peach-colored beaded bolero worn over a regular tank top. A handful of T-shirts were covered with Hannah's face, but otherwise logos and literal references to Hannah were kept to a minimum." Said Disney's Donna Sheridan, "It's not a costume. A tween girl isn't doing dress up, they want to look like they could be Hannah Montana's friend. This is a fashion line."

JULY 2007
♥ *Hannah Montana 2/Meet Miley Cyrus* debuted at the #1 slot on three *Billboard*

charts: the Top 200, Soundtrack and Children's. Responding to the CD's success, the *Los Angeles Times* observed, "Disney Music's strategy has been to court an audience that its larger rivals have mostly ignored — children and preteens whose parents still buy CDs. It's also leveraged the potent partnership it enjoys with the Disney Channel, a veritable launching pad for tween stars. The [CD] epitomizes the approach. 'It's our ability to leverage the synergy of the Walt Disney Company worldwide that has made us the envy and the scourge of the music industry,' [Disney's Gary] Marsh said."

★ Word first started to come out about the fact that there would be a *Hannah Montana* movie released some time in 2008.

✿ An article from the Associated Press Online pointed out, "The week Miley Cyrus debuted on top of the album charts with *Hannah Montana 2/Meet Miley Cyrus*, she appeared on national morning television shows, the cover of *People* magazine, newspaper front pages and other media outlets. The only spot she couldn't be found was the one sure place you would expect a best-selling artist: Top 40 Radio. And she's not alone. A league of tween-leaning acts, including The Cheetah Girls and Aly and AJ, all of whom are current or former stars of the Disney Channel, are routinely mining gold, platinum and multi-platinum CD sales while being virtually locked out of Top 40. That includes songs from the chart-topping soundtrack to *High School Musical*, which was the best-selling album in 2006 and has passed the 4 million mark. 'We had the #1 album of the year and nobody seemed to pay attention in the mainstream radio world; they didn't care,' says Gary Marsh, Disney Worldwide president of entertainment."

AUGUST 2007

❀ Comedy writer Buddy Sheffield, who had written for such TV series as *The Smothers Brothers Show*, *The Dolly Parton Show* and *In Living Color*, filed a lawsuit against Disney claiming that back in 2001 he pitched a series to the Disney Channel called *Rock and Roland*, about a junior high student living a double life as a rock star.

SEPTEMBER 2007

★ Waukesha, Wisconsin, teenager Karli Hintz, who is suffering from a cancerous brain stem tumor, was granted her dream by the Make-A-Wish Foundation, and would be flown out to California so that she could meet her idol, Miley Cyrus. The same was true of Brentwood, Tennessee, teenager Calie Fuqua, fourteen, who was also given the opportunity by Make-A-Wish to go to California and meet Miley.

★ Toward the end of the month, rumors making the rounds were that Miley was dating Nick Jonas, one third of the Jonas Brothers. This was actually one of the first words of a relationship between Miley and anyone else that made it to the media. A few months later, Miley told E! that the only guys in her life she loved were her dad, Jesus and her brothers. Sorry, Nick!

Miley celebrates her win (Choice TV Actress, Comedy) at the 2007 Teen Choice Awards

♥ The speed at which tickets to Miley's concert tour sold out proved to be aggravating to many people — shows were sold out in literally seconds — and this would eventually lead to investigations and a civil lawsuit from members of a Miley fan club, who had been promised the opportunity to purchase tickets.

NOVEMBER 2007

❀ The *Hannah Montana* Fan Club decided that enough bad press was enough and elected to fight back against the people suing them, who were claiming unfair practices that fan club members were shut out from concert tickets. Miley's spokesperson Megan Prophet told MTV, "More than 70,000 MileyWorld members obtained concert tickets as a result of their membership in MileyWorld. MileyWorld members had far greater access to concert tickets than the general public and other fan clubs and the claim that the vast majority of MileyWorld members were unable to obtain concert tickets is simply false." Lawyer Aaron Rihn, representing the civil suit against the fan club, countered, "That's a very small percentage of Miley's actual fan base. That makes it more of a lottery than a realistic benefit of fan-club membership." In a separate story, one woman was so desperate to get her kids tickets to one of the concerts, that she bid $13,000 for a set of four tickets as part of an auction held by radio station WFBQ 94.7 in Indianapolis.

♥ While appearing on *Oprah*, Miley

Miley has nothing but love for her mom and manager, Tish Cyrus, pictured here at the 2006 Teen Choice Awards

admitted that her father was annoyed at her after she had lost a credit card — two days into having it. She also spoke pretty extensively about her life and career. Among the subjects was the way that her dad has kept her grounded ("He's a big influence, not only just because of the music, but growing up around him. I've never seen him treat anyone less than with respect and love, down to the fans that wait until three in the morning until his bus pulls out at five.") and the pressure of being a teen role model ("I say what I'm comfortable in and what I like and nothing that's too out there. I like

Miley and her dad attend the premiere of *High School Musical 2*, which she had a cameo in!

to look kind of like what girls would want to look up to, and their moms and dads will say, 'Hey, that's cool. That's different.' I look way young and that's the way that's more comfortable for me.")

DECEMBER 2007

★ Miley made *Forbes* magazine's 20 Top-Earning Young Superstars Under 25 category. She came in at number 17, earning about $3.5 million a year. The expectation is that she would climb higher in the list during 2008 thanks to the success of the Best of Both Worlds tour.

♥ The *Orange County News* offered up a look at the top-selling toys of the holiday season, among them *Transformers* items and *Hannah Montana* merchandise. "Christmas 2007 might be remembered for the year Monopoly went high-tech," offered the paper, "but you can still tickle Elmo if he isn't overshadowed by Billy Ray Cyrus's daughter . . . The Disney dolls sell for about $20. Some of them sing. They have a fashion collection, a pajama set recommended for ages 6 and up. A DVD game is described as '. . . great for all ages.'"

♥ Due to a phenomenal response in terms of ticket sales, fourteen additional concert dates were added to Miley's schedule of fifty-five. Of the extension, Miley related to the press, "We extended the tour and that's me kind of trying to make sure everyone, especially from my fan club, gets an opportunity to come see the show."

✿ In an interview with jam.canoe.ca, Miley shared her feelings about returning to Toronto, where she had spent some time as her dad shot the series *Doc*. "[Acting] has always been something I wanted to do," she said, "but this is where I started taking classes with [acting teacher] Dean Armstrong. He's incredible. This is where I grew up and this is where I studied so hard, so it's going to be crazy to see everyone."

★ When Miley came to Long Island's Nassau Coliseum, the promoters came up with a unique idea: merchandise went on

sale for people (including non-ticket hold-ers) the afternoon of an evening show.

⭐ Sirius Satellite Radio announced that between December 28, 2007, and January 1, 2008, they would be broadcasting "Miley Radio," which they described as follows: "Miley Radio will feature Miley Cyrus counting down the 45 biggest pop songs in North America in a year-end edition of Sirius Hits 1 Weekend Countdown. Miley will also host special editions of Hit-Bound, Sirius Hits 1's show that uncovers artists and songs that are poised to be the next big thing; and Best of Live Earth Countdown, a recount of the most memorable moments from Live Earth. Miley will also share her personal stories and favorite songs throughout Miley Radio."

🍀 Miley rounded out the year by perform-ing on the ABC broadcast of *Dick Clark's Rockin' New Year's Eve 2008*.

JANUARY 2008

💜 Speaking to *The Detroit News*, Miley was asked whether or not her friends back home were jealous of her success. "I recent-ly asked some of my friends, 'Does being recognized in public make you want to act or not want to?' They said, 'Not want to,' because when they're with me, they realize it's a lot harder being under the glare than they thought." She was also asked if there

Miley and Cyndi Lauper present the award for Best New Artist at the 2008 Grammys

was anyone she'd like to duet with, to which she replied, "Me and Corbin Bleu of *High School Musical* are thinking about doing a song. It's called 'Let's Dance.' That's like my dream. He has a really good voice and he's a really cool guy."

❀ *Animal Fair* magazine named Miley's dogs Roadie and Loco "top dogs." Editor Wendy Diamond explained to *The Dallas Morning News*, "All the time we hear about the sexiest men alive, the best- and worst-dressed celebrities or the most beautiful people. What about the pets?"

★ A bit of controversy erupted over the discovery that Miley uses a body double briefly on stage as she changes from Hannah back to herself. As Miley's representatives told *OK* magazine, "To help speed the transition from Hannah to Miley, there is a production element during the performance of 'We Got the Party' incorporating a body double for Miley. Other than during this very brief transitional moment in the show, Miley performs live during the entirety of both the Hannah and Miley segments of the concert."

♥ Prior to performing in Washington, DC, Miley went to Georgetown University Medical Center and Children's Hospital to visit some sick children, which was coordinated through a charity called Tracy's Kids.

★ Miley's duet with her dad Billy Ray, "Ready, Set, Don't Go," entered the Top 10 at Country Radio.

❀ According to *Entertainment Tonight*, Miley made the nickname the world knows her by official, legally changed her name from Destiny Hope to Miley Ray.

FEBRUARY 2008

♥ The 3D movie version of Miley's Best of Both Worlds tour began selling out as soon as tickets went on sale. There seems to be no end to the Miley phenomenon!

★ With award show season in full swing, Miley appeared as a presenter on the 50th Annual Grammy Awards. Barbara Walters' Oscar Special on February 24 also featured an in-depth interview with Miley who was seen by millions of people around the world when she introduced a song from *Enchanted* at the 80th Annual Academy Awards.

❀ Miley and Billy Ray appeared on *The Tonight Show with Jay Leno* on February 27 where they performed their duet "Ready, Set, Don't Go." Leno got Miley to drink ketchup (she loves it) and Brooke Shields, who plays Miley's mom on *Hannah*, joined them to promote her new show, *Lipstick Jungle*.

MARCH 2008

♥ Miley and her best friend Mandy Jiroux (who is also one of her back-up dancers) had an instant hit with their YouTube show, *The Miley and Mandy Show*, garnering hundreds of thousands of viewers.

★ Miley was one of the youngest people to ever be immortalized in wax when a figure of her was unveiled at New York City's Madame Tussauds museum on March 21.

❀ In a *Grease*-inspired performance, Miley took to the stage of the Nickelodeon Kids' Choice Awards in a smart car and sang "G.N.O." She also picked up trophies for favorite female singer and TV actress.

APRIL 2008

♥ On April 9, Miley joined other celebrities for a special episode of *American Idol*, *Idol Gives Back*, raising money for children in need in the U.S. and around the world.

★ Miley and Billy Ray hosted the CMT Awards on April 14 from their hometown of Nashville, Tennessee. The co-hosts were nominated for the "Tearjerker Video of the Year" award for their duet "Ready, Set, Don't Go."

THE Hannah Montana episode guide

★ SEASON 1 ★

EPISODE 1: "Lilly, Do You Want to Know A Secret?"

Original Air Date: March 24, 2006

Lilly sneaks into Hannah Montana's dressing room after a concert, and learns the truth about Hannah and Miley.

Guest Star: Corbin Bleu plays Johnny Collins, a kid in Miley's school. Miley is nervous around Johnny, who in turn is nervous around Hannah. Corbin Bleu is famous for his roles as Chad Danforth in the *High School Musical* movies, Izzy Daniels in *Jump In!*, and Nathan in the *Flight 29 Down* TV series.

Highlight: Revealing the Hannah Montana closet.

Did You Know?: Fermine (played by Matt Winston) is Hannah's costume designer, and only appears in this first episode.

Did You Notice?: When Miley is rubbing the ketchup off her hands, it disappears and then reappears again. The Hannah wig in this pilot episode is different from the one in the opening, when she sings, "This Is the Life," and the rest of the episodes.

Episode title inspired by: "Do You Want to Know a Secret," most famously recorded by The Beatles

EPISODE 2: "Miley, Get Your Gum"
Original Air Date: March 31, 2006
Oliver is completely obsessed with Hannah Montana, until Miley decides to reveal her secret to him. Jackson buys a "girl car."
Highlight: The "Black Drippage" balloon popping in Oliver's face (which is unnatural, it should have popped in Miley's face).
Did You Know?: The character of Dontzig the Neighbor is named for Gary Dontzig, who co-wrote several episodes.
Did You Notice?: When Lilly says the name of her concert-going alter ego is Lola Lafonda, she actually mouths Lola Luftnagle — the change in dialogue was dubbed over. (In a later episode, she says Lola is the daughter of an oil baron Rudolf Luftnagle.) Also, in the limo, Hannah pulls up her seatbelt onto her shoulder, whereas in the previous shot, the seatbelt was already on her shoulder.
Episode title inspired by: Broadway musical *Annie, Get Your Gun*

EPISODE 3: "She's a Supersneak"
Original Air Date: April 7, 2006
Jackson and Miley are supposed to stay home, but instead they sneak out to see a movie and find Robby on a date. They try to find out more about her, and Miley has to deal with the idea of her father being with someone who is not her mother.
Highlight: The heart-to-heart talk between Robby and Miley. That, or Jackson making his belly button talk (which happens again in future episodes). Or Robby naming a fish "Bucky."
Did You Know?: The song Miley Stewart sings for her late mother (who passed away three years earlier), "I Miss You," was actually written by Miley Cyrus for her late "papi" (grandfather). Robby's date, Margo Diamond, is played by Lindsey Stoddart, who appears on a later episode, "Oh, Say Can You Remember the Words," as a news announcer.
Did You Notice?: When they are behind the cutout for "Little Miss Red Shoes," and a guy comes up to look at it, it switches places in the movie theater, and back again. (Check out

the posters beside the cutout.) Later, Miley is playing an electric guitar, but the sound is that of an acoustic guitar, and she doesn't even strum the last few chords.

Episode title inspired by: "(She's A) Super Freak," recorded by Rick James

EPISODE 4: "I Can't Make You Love Hannah If You Don't"

Original Air Date: April 14, 2006

The only way that Miley's crush, Josh, will reconsider his dislike of Hannah Montana is if Miley goes with him to a Hannah concert. Oliver and Lilly help Miley rush back and forth from the stage to her seat in the audience. Jackson dates his best friend Cooper's sister.

Highlight: Jackson's impersonation of Ozzy Osbourne in sunglasses yelling for Sharon.

Did You Know?: Hannah is on the cover of *Teen Trends* magazine, the same mag of which London and Maddie fight to be on the cover in an episode of *The Suite Life of Zack & Cody*.

Did You Notice?: Jackson doesn't have a job in the previous episode, but now he has a job working at Rico's. The exterior shot of the Hannah concert venue is the Lyric Theater from the *Spider-Man 2* movie, and you can still see a poster of Kirsten Dunst as Mary Jane Watson.

Episode title inspired by: "I Can't Make You Love Me," recorded by Bonnie Raitt

EPISODE 5: "It's My Party and I'll Lie If I Want To"

Original Air Date: April 21, 2006

After Lilly as Lola embarrasses Hannah, Miley tells Lola that a party for singer Kelly Clarkson has been cancelled. But Hannah goes, and ends up with her picture in the paper the next day, which Lilly sees. Jackson goes bald because of a prank set up by Rico.

Highlight: Oliver going long for the football, the first of many times people dive over the ridge at the top of the beach set.

Did You Know?: Traci Van Horn (the socialite played by Romi Dames who appears in several episodes) calls Lilly "Lola Loser Giggles," a reference to Gerty Giggles, the character Emily Osment played in the *Spy Kids* movies. Kelly Clarkson is one of Miley Cyrus's favorite singers. Kay is the name of Hannah's singing coach.

Did You Notice?: When Miley opens the door to presumably let in a skateboarding Lilly, Lilly is standing at the door, and then starts skateboarding. At no point in the episode is Oliver aware that Miley is Hannah. Since the production code for this episode is 102, it aired out of sequence to its creation.

Episode title inspired by: "It's My Party and I'll Cry If I Want To," recorded by Lesley Gore

EPISODE 6: "Grandmas Don't Let Your Babies Grow Up to Play Favorites"

Original Air Date: April 28, 2006

When Robby's mother, Mamaw Ruthie, visits the Stewarts, she favors Jackson over Miley to compensate for the fact that Hannah Montana is always the center of attention. Jackson's volleyball tournament and Hannah's performance for the Queen of England end up in conflict with each other.

Guest Star: Vicki Lawrence plays Mamaw Ruthie Stewart, and also appears in an episode in Season 2. She is famous for her Emmy Award–winning role on the variety series *The Carol Burnett Show*. One of her roles on that show was "Mama," which eventually got spun off into her own series, *Mama's Family*. She was also a singer, with one song — 1970's "The Night the Lights Went Out in Georgia" — reaching #1.

Highlight: The dance competition between Mamaw and Queen Elizabeth.

Did You Know?: Queen Elizabeth II currently has four granddaughters, born in 1981 (Zara Phillips), 1988 (Beatrice), 1990 (Eugenie) and 2003 (Louise). So none of them are the right age for the pre-teen Hannah Montana fan.

Did You Notice?: Oliver is doing the commentating, even though he's in the eighth grade, and Jackson and Topher are playing two-person volleyball for the Seaview Stingrays high school. Also, Jackson touches the net when he spikes, which should have been a fault instead of the winning point.

Episode title inspired by: "Mamas, Don't Let Your Babies Grow Up to Be Cowboys," recorded by Willie Nelson and Waylon Jennings

EPISODE 7: "It's a Mannequin's World"

Original Air Date: May 12, 2006

Miley poses as a mannequin to help Lilly steer Robby towards buying the perfect birthday gift. However, Robby ends up getting a "cat" sweater that Miley has to wear in front of her entire class. Meanwhile, Jackson struggles to keep the birthday cake intact.

Highlight: When Amber and Ashley get cake in the face (they seem to be enjoying it too!).

Did You Know?: Noah Cyrus, Miley's little sister, is the girl who screams at the Miley mannequin, and calls her a freak. This is the first of several times in the series that the writers refer to Billy Ray Cyrus's big hit, "Achy Breaky Heart" when he says "my achy breaky back" doing the limbo. This is Roxy the Bodyguard's (played by Frances Callier) first episode, after returning from a reunion with the Marines.

Did You Notice?: Miley is turning fourteen in this episode, but in the first episode a TV announcer reported that Hannah Montana was fourteen.

Episode title inspired by: "It's a Man's Man's Man's World," recorded by James Brown

EPISODE 8: "Mascot Love"

Original Air Date: May 26, 2006

To spend more time together, Miley and Lilly try out for the school cheerleading squad. Lilly becomes a cheerleader, but

Miley and little sister Noah pose for the cameras at the premiere of *Monster House*, starring Mitchel Musso

Miley ends up team mascot, Pirate Pete. Back at home, Jackson tries to earn some money from Robby by fixing the garbage disposal.

Highlight: Jackson pretending to be Spider-Man in order to escape.

Did You Know?: Miley Cyrus was a competitive cheerleader with the Tennessee All Stars, and said in an interview that she wanted to be a mascot. Seaview Middle School's Pirates were playing Filmore Middle School's Flamingos.

Did You Notice?: Oliver gives out his number twice. Once it's 555-0121, and the other time it's 555-0127.

Episode title inspired by: "Muskrat Love," recorded by Captain and Tennille

EPISODE 9: "Ooh, Ooh, Itchy Woman"

Original Air Date: June 10, 2006

Miley's class goes on a camping trip, and Amber and Ashley take credit for Miley's tent-pitching. Ignoring Robby's warning not to do so, Miley and Lilly take revenge, only to have it backfire on national TV. On the home front, Robby and Jackson attempt to catch Linda, the annoying musical mouse.

Highlight: Lilly's tirade against the "lying evil nasties!"

Did You Know?: Baz Roberts is the fictitious director of at least two of Hannah's videos. Jackson sets 248 traps. Creagen Dow, who plays Oliver's tormentor Donny, went on to have a recurring role as Jeremiah Trottman on Nickelodeon's *Zoey 101*.

Did You Notice?: The rain cover of the tent is yellow in one scene, and then blue in the next.

Episode title inspired by: "Witchy Woman," recorded by the Eagles

EPISODE 10: "Oh Say, Can You Remember the Words?"

Original Air Date: June 30, 2006

When Miley and Oliver have to do a scene from *Romeo and Juliet* for drama class, Miley tries to help Oliver get over stage fright. Then Miley forgets the words to the national anthem and even her own songs on national TV, until Oliver steps in to help her. Meanwhile, Jackson binges on candy after stopping Rico from eating some.

Highlight: The chocolate bunny terrorizing Jackson on the couch.

Did You Know?: Noah Cyrus appears again as the kid who drops the ice cream cone. "Beary" is the name of Miley's teddy bear, but is also the name of the character that Emily's brother, Haley Joel Osment, voiced on *The Country Bears*.

Did You Notice?: Lilly flips the cue cards from the "Throw My Cares" card to the "This Is The Life" card, but in the next shot, it's back to the "Throw My Cares" card. Lilly loves "Top Rockers" but remember from last episode, Taylor Kingsford is her favorite.

Episode title inspired by: "The Star Spangled Banner"

EPISODE 11: "Oops! I Meddled Again"

Original Air Date: July 14, 2006

When Hannah Montana receives fan mail from Becca Weller (played by Kirby Bliss Blanton) revealing that she has a crush on Oliver, Miley, Lilly and Robby help Oliver get over his nerves to ask her out. Meanwhile, Rico forces Jackson to wear a chicken suit to promote Rico's chicken wings.

Highlight: Miley parasailing in a chicken suit to stop Oliver from breaking up with Becca.

Did You Know?: Oliver's full name is Oliver Oscar Oken, which leads to the nicknames Ollie Trolley, Smokin' Oken and Triple O. Becca Weller is the second person that Oliver "Locker Man" Oken helped out in "Miley, Get Your Gum."

Did You Notice?: This episode has a production code of 107, and in it Robby is working on the song, "The Other Side of Me," which is performed by Hannah in earlier episodes. Also, check out Oliver's backpack in the locker scene where he talks about the date: it jumps from his hand, back to his shoulder and then on the floor. Oliver's locker is on the other side of the hall from earlier episodes.

Episode title inspired by: "Oops! . . . I Did It Again," recorded by Britney Spears

EPISODE 12: "On the Road Again"

Original Air Date: July 28, 2006

Miley arranges a comeback for Robby Ray's rock-and-roll career, leaving Roxy to look after Jackson and Miley. This was a cross-over episode with *That's So Raven* and *The Suite Life of*

Zack & Cody, in which Hannah Montana shows up at the Tipton, and meets Raven Baxter and the Tipton gang. She orders a dress from Raven, licks vanilla cake (her favorite) from Cody's shirt and tries to collect on her payment from performing at London's birthday party.

Guest Star: Ashley Tisdale plays Maddie, the character she plays on *The Suite Life of Zack & Cody*. Ashley is also famous for her role as Sharpay Evans in *High School Musical* and *High School Musical 2*. Maddie fawns over Robby Ray, her mother's favorite singer.

Highlight: Jackson's musical talent of playing the underarm (and underknee) trumpet.

Did You Know?: Billy Ray Cyrus sang "I Want My Mullet Back" (a song he was working on at the time) in an audition with Miley. Billy Ray also released his album *Wanna Be Your Joe*, with the "Mullet" song a week before this episode aired.

Did You Notice?: In the scene where they watch "Robbypalooza" (which is old footage of Billy Ray performing), Miley's sweater switches from buttoned to unbuttoned back to buttoned.

Episode title inspired by: "On the Road Again," recorded by Willie Nelson

EPISODE 13: "You're So Vain, You Probably Think This Zit Is About You"
Original Air Date: August 12, 2006
Miley convinces Lilly that looks don't matter when she needs to wear glasses for a skateboarding competition. However, Miley gets rid of a zit on a new Hannah billboard, and Lilly finds out. Meanwhile, Jackson has to wear a dress to be Rico's assistant in a magic show, to get a raise.

Highlight: Lilly high-fiving Miley's forehead.

Did You Know?: Gina DeVivo, who plays Lilly's rival, Heather, was one of the final six actresses auditioning for the role of Lilly. The photographer, Liza, plays Samantha Samuels in Disney Channel's *Cory in the House*. Jackson's love interest Melissa is played by *Friday Night Lights'* Aimee Teegarden.

Did You Notice?: When Miley covers her face with a scarf, it falls off; in the next shot, she's taking it off.

Episode title inspired by: "You're So Vain," recorded by Carly Simon

EPISODE 14: "New Kid in School"
Original Air Date: August 18, 2006
When everyone is sucking up to TV star Jake Ryan (played by Cody Linley), Miley decides to reveal the truth about her other identity to TV reporter Bree Yung Zhusdan Takahashi Samuels (played by Geraldine Yeo), but then has to convince the reporter that she is a

deluded fan who only *thinks* she's Hannah. Meanwhile, Jackson makes Robby pay for allowing his car door to get torn off.

Highlight: Jackson as Elvis, and Robby introducing himself as Billy Ray Cyrus, sporting a mullet wig.

Did You Know?: Jake Ryan is the name of the heart-throb in the movie *Sixteen Candles*. An eyeliner pencil was used to make the scratch on Robby's new Porsche convertible.

Did You Notice?: Jackson's full name is Jackson Rod Stewart. Rod Stewart is a singer, whose most famous hit was "Do Ya Think I'm Sexy?"

Episode title inspired by: "New Kid in Town," recorded by the Eagles

EPISODE 15: "More Than a Zombie to Me"

Original Air Date: September 8, 2006

Miley rejects Jake's invitation to the '70s dance, though she has a change of heart when she appears on Jake's TV show, *Zombie High*, and during the course of their conversation learns that he actually has feelings for a girl named Miley. But when Jake asks Lilly, the two girls end up fighting over him at the dance. Meanwhile, Robby and Jackson try to outprank each other.

Highlight: Brushing Demon Dog's teeth in preparation for a kiss with Hannah Montana.

Did You Know?: Jake's TV show, *Zombie High*, is a parody of *Buffy the Vampire Slayer*, with Jake as the Slayer, and Hannah Montana as his undead girlfriend (similar to Angel). When Jackson pulls the cake prank, he says "Boo-yah." This was Cyborg's classic line from *Teen Titans*, and Cyborg was voiced by Khary Payton, who plays Roger the Director in this episode.

Did You Notice?: The *Zombie High* set is actually the bathroom set, used at the start and end of the episode.

Episode title inspired by: "More Than a Woman to Me," recorded by the Bee Gees

EPISODE 16: "Good Golly, Miss Dolly"

Original Air Date: September 29, 2006

Aunt Dolly comes to visit, and Miley shares everything that's been happening in her life. Unfortunately, Aunt Dolly's video camera records her admission that she is in love with Jake Ryan, and Oliver unknowingly hands it over to Jake. Then it's up to Aunt Dolly, Miley and Lilly to steal it back. Meanwhile, Robby and Jackson try to reclaim their manhood.

Guest Star: Dolly Parton plays Aunt Dolly. She is a country music legend, and has starred in such films as *Rhinestone* and *9 to 5*.

Highlight: When Lilly wants to borrow Hannah's cute purse.

Did You Know?: In real life, Dolly Parton is Miley Cyrus's godmother.

Did You Notice?: Miley runs out of the house with the video camera, but when she gets to school, she's also wearing a flowered jacket. Also, when Miley steals the videotapes, the stacks keep changing, and there's a shot of the tapes right before she steals them that's the shot *after* she steals them.

Episode title inspired by: "Good Golly, Miss Molly," recorded by Little Richard

119

EPISODE 17: "Torn Between Two Hannahs"

Original Air Date: October 14, 2006

Miley's look-alike cousin, Luann (played by Miley Cyrus), is in town from Tennessee. Luann locks Miley in a closet, and sets out to reveal Miley's secret at a Hannahween concert. Robby and Jackson try to be scarier than their neighbor for Halloween.

Highlight: Jackson taking the rented pony to his room.

Did You Know?: "Stand" is on Billy Ray Cyrus's album *Wanna Be Your Joe*. When Lilly whispers, ". . . she sees dead people," it's a reference to the line Emily Osment's brother made famous in *The Sixth Sense*. Miley Cyrus's little sister, Noah, is one of the Halloween children.

Did You Notice?: Dontzig grabs the pot of candy as he runs away from the two Stewarts, but then as the scene goes on with the credits, the pot of candy reappears.

Episode title inspired by: "Torn Between Two Lovers," recorded by Mary MacGregor

EPISODE 18: "People Who Use People"

Original Air Date: November 3, 2006

Miley uses a boy to make Jake jealous, but he turns out to be younger than she thought. Jake also uses a film co-star to make Miley jealous, and when they confront each other, they end up kissing. Meanwhile, Jackson makes Robby go out with his teacher in the hopes of a better grade.

Highlight: Lilly falling backwards off her chair when she sees the kiss, with the popcorn flying.

Did You Know?: Miley Cyrus said on Radio Disney that this was her favorite episode.

Did You Notice?: The guy at the pretzel stand gives Miley a pretzel without her asking or paying for it. Also, outside the bowling alley a sign reads Parkway Lanes, but inside the place is called Malibu Lanes. (That's because the exterior shot was also used in *The Suite Life of Zack & Cody* episode "Bowling.")

Episode title inspired by: "People," recorded by Barbra Streisand

EPISODE 19: "Money for Nothing, Guilt for Free"

Original Air Date: November 26, 2006

Miley, Lilly and Oliver set out to beat Amber and Ashley at raising money for United People's Relief (which is always used as "the charity" in this series), by getting Hannah Montana to do the fundraising. Then, since Sarah plans to give the prize of $300 in clothing to needy children, they try to give Sarah the money. Meanwhile, Jackson gets good at Ping-Pong in order to beat his dad at a sport.

Highlight: Jackson falling to the onslaught of Ping-Pong balls from Cooper's gun.

Did You Know?: The little girl who was in the ball pit is Noah Cyrus. Morgan York, who played Sarah, was one of the kids in the *Cheaper by the Dozen* movies.

Did You Notice?: The money that Oliver is holding after the Hannah Montana concert is marked "Motion Picture Use Only." All of the water that Jackson and Robby drink is Dasani.

Episode title inspired by: "Money For Nothing," recorded by Dire Straits

EPISODE 20: "Debt It Be"

Original Air Date: December 1, 2006

When Miley racks up the charges on her "emergency" credit card, Jackson convinces her to sell off Hannah Montana stuff to pay off the card. But when she sells borrowed sapphire earrings to an old lady, Jackson has to dress up as Hannah's grandmother to get them back.

Highlight: Jackson as Nana Montana, talking about Abraham Lincoln.

Did You Know?: Miley Cyrus said her worst fear is spiders, which is why Miley Stewart doesn't want to clean out the garage in this episode. Also, Miley Cyrus revealed on *Oprah* that her dad gave her a credit card, and she lost it after two days.

Did You Notice?: When Miley is looking at the skirt in the flea market, her purse disappears and then reappears on her left elbow.

Episode title inspired by: "Let It Be," recorded by The Beatles

EPISODE 21: "My Boyfriend's Jackson and There's Gonna Be Trouble"

Original Air Date: January 1, 2007

A paparazzo named Paulie takes a photo of Hannah Montana with Jackson, and Jacksannah is born! But Jackson doesn't want to give up the relationship once he sees the free stuff he's given. Finally Hannah breaks up with Jackson on a talk show, but not before Jackson redeems himself. Meanwhile, Oliver and Sarah are the proud parents of a sack of flour.

Highlight: Robby Ray asking Jackson why he's not breaking up with his sister.

Did You Know?: "Tomkat" is the nickname given to the couple, Tom Cruise and Katie Holmes. When Jackson is jumping on the couch, it's a spoof of Tom Cruise jumping on the couch on *Oprah*, professing his love for Katie.

Did You Notice?: This is the first episode where Miley/Hannah never appears with Lilly. Traci's cat is named Madonna.

Episode title inspired by: "My Boyfriend's Back," recorded by The Angels

EPISODE 22: "We Are Family: Now Get Me Some Water!"

Original Air Date: January 7, 2007

When Miley asks Rico for a raise for Jackson, he fires him. So Hannah hires Jackson as her assistant. But when he keeps screwing up, including injuring a dancer and subbing for him,

she fires him, and sweet-talks Rico into hiring him again.

Highlight: Hannah and Jackson in the boxing ring for the "I Got Nerve" performance.

Did You Know?: This episode aired just five days before the Disney Channel premiered *Jump In!*, also set in part in a boxing gym. Also, Miley uses her dad's old nickname for her, Smiley Miley, in this episode.

Did You Notice?: Miley lifts Rico off the ground with her left hand, but then she's moving her left hand and Rico's still at the same height. Also in this episode, Lola's last name is LaToya, but she's also sporting a new orange wig.

Episode title inspired by: "We Are Family," recorded by Sister Sledge

EPISODE 23: "Schooly Bully"
Original Air Date: January 19, 2007
Miley gets picked on by a new kid, "The Cracker," and Roxy tells her to go to the principal about it. When she doesn't, Roxy shows up as an even meaner bully, and makes Miley and Lilly's life difficult until they finally tell the principal. Meanwhile, Robby and Jackson decide to male-bond on a fishing trip but they get stuck with a strange ventriloquist motel owner (played by Kenneth Mars, best known for his roles in the films of Mel Brooks).

Highlight: Jackson plowing himself in the wall of snow blocking the door.

Did You Know?: This is the first episode where Robby and Miley/Hannah don't have a scene together. Principal Marsh is the new principal of Seaview Middle School, after Principal Fisher retired in the episode "Good Golly, Miss Dolly."

Did You Notice?: Lilly says the name of the cute boy who asks Miley and Lilly to a party is Troy McCann, but the credits name him Troy Cole.

EPISODE 24: "The Idol Side of Me"

Original Air Date: February 9, 2007

When they are at the bottom of Amber and Ashley's "Cool" list, Miley and Lilly decide to embarrass Amber on the show *Singing With the Stars*. But when Amber promises to be nicer at school, Hannah Montana gets covered in green gook instead. Meanwhile, Robby and Jackson tries to shut up their neighbor Dontzig's dog, Oscar.

Highlight: Amber's two spit-takes (a "spit-take" is when a character sprays out food or drink).

Did You Know?: This episode was directed by Fred Savage, known for playing Kevin Arnold on the TV series *The Wonder Years*, and the little boy in *The Princess Bride*. Roger S. Christiansen actually directed fifteen of the twenty-six episodes in the first season. Also, Oscar is the same dog as Ivana, London's dog in *The Suite Life of Zack & Cody*. Ashley sings *terribly* but actress Anna Marie Perez is a great singer in real life.

Did You Notice?: Robby is writing the song "If We Were A Movie," but Aunt Dolly, Miley and Robby sang it already in an earlier episode (made just before this one). Also, Amber brags at school about winning on the show "last night" but earlier she said the show would be on Saturday.

Episode title inspired by: "The Other Side of Me," recorded by Hannah Montana

EPISODE 25: "Smells Like a Teen Sellout"

Original Air Date: March 2, 2007

Hannah Montana sponsors a perfume that she hates (because it smells like raspberries, which make her sick) in order to keep the gifts including a car. She tries to lie about it during a TV interview but she adopts everyone else's nervous habits when lying, including giggling and sweating. Meanwhile, Jackson auditions for Teen Wilderness Challenge.

Highlight: Hannah spitting out "sweat" on Colin Lassiter's show.

Did You Know?: Ryan Newman, the girl who plays Young Miley in this and the "I Am Hannah, Hear Me Croak" episodes, was one of the voices in *Monster House*, along with Mitchel Musso. Maria the Car is a Ford Mustang convertible, but with the emblem painted black so as not to be identifiable.

Did You Notice?: Before shooting the perfume commercial, Hannah hands Lola the fake perfume, and then in the next shot, she hands it to her again. In the interview, Hannah's glass of water disappears and reappears.

Episode title inspired by: "Smells Like Teen Spirit," recorded by Nirvana

EPISODE 26: "Bad Moose Rising"

Original Air Date: March 30, 2007

Jackson is frustrated at driving Miley everywhere, thanklessly. So he bets Miley she couldn't take care of Dontzig's annoying niece, Patty (played by Savannah Stehlin), for a day without complaining. They end up at Make-A-Moose, where Miley rushes Patty so that she can get to a fashion show where Lilly has said that she could model and keep a Stella Fabione dress. Meanwhile, Roxy tries to clear Robby's sinuses.

Highlight: Miley filling (and exploding) her pants with moose stuffing.

Did You Know?: The Make-A-Moose store is based on the Build-A-Bear Workshop. Bullwinkle was an animated moose in an early '60s cartoon. Douglas Lieblein, who co-wrote this episode, had the most writing credits (five of them) in the first season, along with Sally Lapiduss (five credits), Heather Wordham (four), Todd J. Greenwald (three), and Michael Poryes (three).

Did You Notice?: When they're at the beach, Oliver has chocolate all over his face, and then in the next shot, the chocolate is gone.

Episode title inspired by: "Bad Moon Rising," recorded by Creedence Clearwater Revival

★ SEASON 2 ★

EPISODE 1: "Me and Rico Down by the School Yard"

Original Air Date: April 23, 2007

On the first day of high school, Rico takes a cellphone photo that could reveal Miley's "secret." He forces Miley to be his girlfriend, while Lilly and Oliver try to steal the phone. Miley finally tells Rico to reveal it anyway, only to find out that the secret was that Miley had brought Beary to school. Meanwhile, Jackson reluctantly befriends Thor, a new kid from Minnesota.

Highlight: Robby's "At Home Without Kids" song.

Did You Know?: In this first episode of the second season, Moises Arias is billed in the show's opening credits, as Rico has now "skipped a few grades" and joined Miley's freshman class at Seaview High School. This was the first of five episodes that aired on consecutive nights, billed by Disney Channel as "Hannah Montana's Freshman High-Five."

Did You Notice?: When Miley kisses Beary, she kisses him on the left side of the face. But in Rico's photo, Miley is kissing Beary's right ear. Jackson's friend says that Jackson came to Malibu from Tennessee two years ago (when he was a freshman, and now he's a junior), but in "It's A Mannequin's World," we learn that the Stewarts have been in the Malibu house for at least three years.

Episode title inspired by: "Me and Julio Down By the Schoolyard," recorded by Paul Simon

EPISODE 2: "Cuffs Will Keep Us Together"
Original Air Date: April 24, 2007
Miley and Lilly are fighting because Lilly wouldn't pick Miley for her flag football team. So Oliver handcuffs them together, but loses the key. Still handcuffed when Hannah Montana has to accept an award on national TV for her song "True Friend," they both realize what true friendship means. Meanwhile, Robby gives Jackson the silent treatment to get him to do chores.
Highlight: When Robby finally talks to Jackson after he puts pistachio pudding in the cake.
Did You Know?: Oliver says he'd love to go surfing with sharks, but in an interview with Mitchel Musso, he said his worst fear is sharks. Robby says that Carrie Underwood introduced Hannah Montana; at the 2007 CMA Awards, it was Miley Cyrus introducing Carrie Underwood. Though it aired second, this was the first episode of the second season to be shot.
Did You Notice?: When Lilly has her feet on Miley's shoulders, their wrists are not

handcuffed though they should be. Jackson's arm is clean when the tattoo artist starts with the needle, but a professional tattoo artist would draw the design first.

Episode title inspired by: "Love Will Keep Us Together," recorded by Captain & Tennille

EPISODE 3: "You Are So Sue-able to Me"

Original Air Date: April 25, 2007

Miley gives Lilly a "girl" makeover when Matt Marshal asks her to a dance, but preferring the tomboy Lilly, he stands her up. Upset, Lilly and Miley sue Matt on the TV show *Teen Court*. When the judge learns of Miley's interference, Miley gets the justice. Meanwhile, Jackson has to decide between Robby and new friend Thor to take to the Lakers playoff game.

Highlight: Jackson sitting on whoopee cushions to convince Robby that the burrito was giving him gas.

Did You Know?: Oliver isn't in this episode — it's the first time one of the main cast members doesn't appear. The outside shots of the school are of John F. Kennedy High School in Granada Hills, Los Angeles.

Did You Notice?: Despite being into each other, Lilly's love interest Matt Marshal (played by Bubba Lewis) never comes back. In the scene at Rico's shack, Lilly has a braid with a loop that disappears and reappears. The right-most cushion on the couch didn't have a whoopee cushion under it, but it still makes a noise when Jackson and Thor sit on it.

Episode title inspired by: "You Are So Beautiful," recorded by Billy Preston, made popular by Joe Cocker

EPISODE 4: "Get Down, Study-udy-udy"

Original Air Date: April 26, 2007

If Miley doesn't get a good grade on her biology mid-term, then she's not allowed to go on her European tour. So she creates a Bone Dance to memorize the names of 206 bones, and eventually gets an A because of the study technique. Meanwhile, when Jackson takes care of Thor's parrot, he wrecks his study date with Becky.

Highlight: Oliver's nosebleed.

Did You Know?: *Goodnight Moon* (the parrot's favorite book) was the first book Miley Cyrus ever read. Robby is going to teach the parrot "I Wanna Be Your Joe," which is the title song of Billy Ray's 2006 album.

Did You Notice?: Ms. Kunkle (played by Erin Matthews) teaches Miley biology, but she taught Jackson math. Rico's art class was in a history classroom (there's a sign on the door).

When Miley is doing the Bone Dance, in subsequent shots Rico is looking at the tests, then dancing on the chair, then looking at the tests again. And how can Miley be cheating by signaling answers if she's the last person writing the test?

Episode title inspired by: "Boogie Oogie Oogie" recorded by A Taste of Honey

EPISODE 5: "I Am Hannah, Hear Me Croak"

Original Air Date: April 27, 2007

First, Miley can't speak for a week to get over laryngitis. Then, she has to have surgery to repair her voice, but Miley is scared that she'll be the one in a million whose voice is ruined by it. In a dream, Miley's mom reassures her that she'll still have loving friends and family, no matter what happens.

Guest Star: Brooke Shields plays Miley's mom in the dream sequence. Brooke is a supermodel who came to fame with the movies *Pretty Baby* and *Blue Lagoon*, and has since starred in several movies and TV series, including *Suddenly Susan* (the connection to *Hannah Montana*'s executive producer, Steve Peterman). Brooke's grandmother was an Italian princess!

Highlight: Jackson dancing with the multi-colored pants, pretending it's Jenny.

Did You Know?: Lilly tickles Miley to get her to drop a lollipop. In real life, tickling is one of the things Miley Cyrus hates the most (as she revealed on the soundtrack CD). Billy Ray Cyrus brings his kids hot chocolate when they're sick or feeling sad. The young Miley and Jackson are both played by Ryans (Newman and Adkisson).

Did You Notice?: Even though it was the Loco Hot Cocoa that caused the dream, Miley doesn't even drink it. When on the beach, Miley's marker jumps from the board to her hand to the board again.

Episode title inspired by: "I Am Woman," recorded by Helen Reddy

EPISODE 6: "You Gotta Not Fight for Your Right to Party"

Original Air Date: May 4, 2007

Miley and Jackson have to share a bathroom, and the bickering gets too much for Robby despite family meetings and padded combat. So he grounds them, even though they both

have evening plans. They convince Lilly and Oliver to take their place, while they go out. They drive Thor's borrowed truck to the edge of a cliff, and have to work together to save themselves.

Highlight: Lilly getting a Robby Ray autograph for her Uncle Wilhelm von Kurankardenstate.

Did You Know?: Panic at the Disco (the band that Jackson is going to see) had only one album out when this episode was made, *A Fever You Can't Sweat Out*, with the hit single, "I Write Sins Not Tragedies."

Did You Notice?: At the beginning of the episode, Miley can't get water out of the faucet because Jackson is using the shower, but then later in the scene, she can get water. Also, the kids have separate bathrooms, but earlier (in the "Oops! I Meddled Again" episode) the kids only had one bathroom.

Episode title inspired by: "(You Gotta) Fight For Your Right (to Party)," recorded by the Beastie Boys

EPISODE 7: "My Best Friend's Boyfriend"

Original Air Date: May 18, 2007

Miley is not liking the dewy-eyed relationship between Lilly and her new boyfriend, Lucas, but she's *really* not liking it when she catches him kissing another girl. However, Lilly won't believe her. So as Hannah, she flirts with him in a restaurant to convince Lilly, who watches on as Lola. Meanwhile, Jackson gets tied up and deep-freezed, all because of Rico's new alarm system.

Guest Stars: Larry David as himself. Larry was the co-creator of the TV series *Seinfeld*, and the creator and star of the TV series *Curb Your Enthusiasm*. Also, **Austin Butler**, who plays Derek, Miley's "Worst Date of Her Life," has gone on to have a starring role in Nickelodeon's *Zoey 101* (replacing Sean Flynn) and is in the movie *They Came From Upstairs* with Ashley Tisdale, slated for a 2009 release.

Highlight: Derek freaking out when Robby comes in with a chainsaw.

Did You Know?: Larry David and his two daughters, Romy and Cazzie, waiting over an hour to get a table at the Chinese restaurant is a play on a famous *Seinfeld* episode (where Jerry, George and Elaine do the same). The joke continues when the daughter says, "Maybe Uncle Jerry could get us in." Larry David apparently wanted to be on the show because his daughters were big *Hannah Montana* fans. Frances Callier, who plays Hannah's bodyguard Roxy, acted in an episode of *Curb Your Enthusiasm*.

Did You Notice?: Miley's "Movie Jammies" are the ones that Lilly borrowed and wore when she slept over in the episode "You Are So Sue-Able to Me."

Episode title inspired by: "My Best Friend's Girl," recorded by The Cars

EPISODE 8: "Take This Job and Love It"

Original Air Date: June 16, 2007

Frustrated at Roxy ruining her dates, Miley suggests that Roxy get a job providing security to the President. Later Miley regrets her suggestion, and Hannah and Lola visit the President's daughter so that Miley can apologize to Roxy. But first she has to cure Humphrey, the President's dog. Meanwhile, Jackson pretends to be a motocross racer to impress Julie.

Highlight: Lilly being Hannah Montana.

Did You Know?: This was a crossover episode with Disney's *Cory in the House*, with John Aquino as the President, and Madison Pettis as Sophie, his daughter. The "Dog Whisperer" is the nickname of Cesar Millan, who has had his own show on National Geographic Channel since 2004. The fictional store, Make A Moose, is mentioned again.

Did You Notice?: In "Good Golly, Miss Dolly," Miley says she modeled Hannah's look after Aunt Dolly, but in this episode it was Roxy who picked out the wig when Miley was shopping at Wig City. Also, when Miley is eating the dog food, her face is clean, and then when Roxy recognizes Miley, her chin is covered in sauce.

Episode title inspired by: "Take This Job and Shove It," recorded by Johnny Paycheck

EPISODE 9: "Achey Jakey Heart, Part 1"

Original Air Date: June 24, 2007

Jake Ryan returns from Romania, tries to win back Miley's heart and does so when he inadvertently tells a TV reporter that he loves Miley. To not have any secrets between them, Miley tells Jake that she is Hannah Montana. Meanwhile, Jackson and Oliver create a Cheese Jerky shack to compete with Rico's overpriced food.

Highlight: The Cheese Jerky rap by Oliver and Jackson.

Did You Know?: Brian Winters, the TV reporter (played by Brandon Johnson), is also the host of *Singing With the Stars* in "The Idol Side of Me" episode. Emily Osment likes her steak medium rare.

Did You Notice?: When Lilly is looking at the tabloid mag telling Miley about Jake's return, she is looking at different articles without ever flipping pages. Plus Jake was gone for six months making *Teen Gladiators and the Sword of Fire*, when he told Miley in "People Who Use People" that he would be gone for four months.

Episode title inspired by: "Achy Breaky Heart," recorded by Billy Ray Cyrus

EPISODE 10: "Achey Jakey Heart, Part 2"

Original Air Date: June 24, 2007

When Jake adopts the alter ego Milos to hang out with Miley and her friends privately, they discover that he's still obnoxious. Afraid that Jake will reveal Hannah's secret, Miley tries to get Jake to break up with her, but ends up breaking up with him. Meanwhile, when Jackson's shack is not profitable, he pretends getting fired from Rico's never happened.

Highlight: Jackson pulling Rico into the cheese pot, and then Rico eating it with the jerky.

Did You Know?: The little girl whose drink Jake takes is Noah Cyrus. The dress that Miley wears on the red carpet is a copy of the swan dress worn by Björk to the 2001 Academy Awards. Robby says, "Good night, Nurse Nichol"; Nurse Nichol was a main character in the series *Doc*, which Billy Ray starred in before *Hannah Montana*. (See page 24 for a pic of the actress who played Nurse Nichol; she's sitting on the bed.)

Did You Notice?: If Jake is seen going out with Hannah instead of Miley, then it will be all over the papers. But if Miley is seen going out with Milos instead of Jake, no one will notice.

Episode title inspired by: "Achy Breaky Heart," recorded by Billy Ray Cyrus

EPISODE 11: "Sleepwalk This Way"

Original Air Date: July 7, 2007

Robby has written a new song for Hannah, but won't play it until he gets his lucky guitar back. Miley finds the "song" about bunnies and she hates it. Jackson convinces her to keep quiet so that he can finally have a party at the house, but Miley sleepwalks when she's keeping a secret. It turns out that this wasn't the song, but a song Miley wrote when she was five years old.

Highlight: Oliver asking Ms. Kunkle to marry him.

Did You Know?: When Robby is sleeping, he says, "One, two, cha-cha-cha. I pulled the mullet, mother, but it just wouldn't come off." When Billy Ray was on *Dancing With the Stars*, he was supposed to take a mullet wig off his partner's head, but it got stuck. That was the movie *The Wizard of Oz* that Jackson was crying while watching.

Did You Notice?: In the episode "Torn Between Two Hannahs," Miley says that Robby uses a new song to soften bad news, but in this episode a new song means that everyone is in a great mood. Also, Robby sang the new song in the "Two Hannahs" episode on a guitar other than Lucky Lulu, which in this episode he says he never does. Also, we can see that Miley never hits her head (despite the sound effect) when Jackson is carrying her inside the house.

Episode title inspired by: "Walk This Way," recorded by Aerosmith

EPISODE 12: "When You Wish You Were the Star"

Original Air Date: July 13, 2007

Forced to work on her science project instead of going out with Jesse McCartney, Miley wishes on a falling star that she was Hannah Montana all the time. It comes true. Her Angel (played by Frances Callier) shows her that, in this life, her dad has re-married, her friends don't know her and Jackson hates her. When Jackson wishes for his old life back, things return to normal.

Guest Star: Jesse McCartney plays himself. Jesse is a recording artist, portrayed Adam on *All My Children*, Bradin Westerly on *Summerland* and provides his voice for the character of Theodore in *Alvin and the Chipmunks*.

Highlight: Jesse McCartney telling Hannah that she's so cute while she kicks him out.

Did You Know?: Hannah was on *Circus With the Stars*, which is not only another reference to *Dancing With the Stars*, but *Circus of the Stars* was an annual variety show (1977–1994) where celebrities would perform circus acts. When the Angel wears Viking horns and a big clock around her neck while Jesse, Rico and Oliver rap and break-dance, this is a hip-hop homage to Flavor Flav. The whole show is a take on the classic movie *It's*

A Wonderful Life, featuring another Stewart, Jimmy.

Did You Notice?: In Hannah's bedroom, the Hannah Moosetana from the "Bad Moose Rising" episode is on her night-table. In the beach scene, you can see the studio lights in the sunglasses of Hannah, Oliver and Rico. The Loco Hot Cocoa appears again, perhaps to explain this all as a dream?

Episode title inspired by: "When You Wish Upon a Star," from Disney's *Pinocchio*

EPISODE 13: "I Want You to Want Me . . . to Go to Florida"

Original Air Date: July 21, 2007

A new pop star, Mikayla, trash-talks Hannah Montana before they both are to appear at a charity concert in Florida. When Robby puts his back and neck out, he refuses to let Miley fly to Florida with Roxy instead of him. Miley goes anyway, and Robby and Jackson have to chase after her. With Jackson's help, Robby tells Miley he's having a hard time letting her grow up.

Guest Stars: Selena Gomez plays Mikayla. Selena was Gianna in *Barney & Friends*, in *Spy Kids 3D* with Emily Osment, and has subsequently gone on to star as Alex Russo in the Disney Channel series *The Wizards of Waverly Place*, and is rumored to play the role of Tiara in *High School Musical 3*. **Camryn Manheim** plays Margot, Mikayla's manager. Camryn starred in the TV series *The Practice* and *Ghost Whisperer*.

Highlight: Rico flying through the air after trying Jackson's exercise machine.

Did You Know?: The episode reveals Miley's full name to be Miley Ray Stewart. Miley Cyrus changed her real name from Destiny Hope to Miley Ray in 2008. Mikayla's song, "If Cupid Had A Heart," was written by Gordon Pogoda, and sung by Julie Griffin (and can only be bought online).

Did You Notice?: Miley is really bad at football ("Cuffs Will Keep Us Together"), but she hits Rico with a perfect throw. Also, it's the same sky outside the airplane when it's on the ground as when it's in the air.

Episode title inspired by: "I Want You to Want Me," recorded by Cheap Trick

EPISODE 14: "Everybody Was Best Friend Fighting"
Original Air Date: August 4, 2007
After Oliver adopts his alter ego Mike Standley III to hang out with Hannah, she is invited to play in a charity tennis tournament. Oliver and Lilly fight over the one ticket she gets until Rico (being nice, because Jackson tricked him into being nice so he could get some time off) gives up a second ticket. Even then, the friends fight so much at the game that Hannah plays poorly.
Highlight: Oliver showing up to the concert in his Dracula Halloween costume.
Did You Know?: The fortune teller was played by Karina Smirnoff, Billy Ray's dance partner on *Dancing With the Stars*. After Robby says he's not much of a dancer, the fortune teller says, "I know, but if you would just bend your knees," and later says, "Now, you move your feet!" These were the judges' main complaints about Billy Ray's dancing. Also, the little girl with the ice cream that needed a napkin? Once again, Miley's little sister, Noah.
Did You Notice?: When Oliver is asking to come backstage at the beginning of the show, Hannah has a silver purse on her right shoulder that keeps disappearing and reappearing, depending on the shot. Also, when the second caramel apple lands on Rico's head, the first caramel apple is in a different position than before the second apple landed.
Episode title inspired by: "Kung Fu Fighting," recorded by Carl Douglas

EPISODE 15: "Song Sung Bad"
Original Air Date: August 4, 2007
Miley and Robby re-mix Lilly's voice for a birthday CD for her mom. Thinking she sounds great, Lilly challenges Amber to a karaoke competition. When Lilly learns the truth, they decide to use Miley's voice instead. After Miley tangles with a spider in the middle of the song, she has to convince Lilly and her friends that singing should be fun, no matter how you sound. Meanwhile, Jackson has to win Sarah's heart for Rico, but Sarah thinks it's Jackson who's crushing on her.
Highlight: Rico and Jackson battling Rs with "Sarah" and "Rosalita."
Did You Know?: The CD that Lilly gives to her mother has Emily Osment's actual singing voice. It must have been a tough scene to have a tarantula crawl on her body if Miley Cyrus's worst fear is spiders.
Did You Notice?: After Miley stomps on Oliver's foot the first time, she glances at the camera a couple of times (was someone laughing?). When Rico gulps the last strawberry milk shot, no one was there to pour it. When Lilly does the do-over, she starts singing "Life's

What You Make It," not re-doing "I've Got Nerve." Also, in the episode "Get Down, Study-udy-udy," Lilly and Oliver sing well, and in this episode, they suck.
Episode title inspired by: "Song Sung Blue," recorded by Neil Diamond

EPISODE 16: "Me and Mr. Jonas and Mr. Jonas and Mr. Jonas"
Original Air Date: August 18, 2007
When Robby hangs out with the Jonas Brothers while writing a song for them, Miley gets jealous. So she and Lilly disguise themselves as another boy-band to make the guys think that Robby stole the song, and of course they're found out. Meanwhile, Rico helps Jackson break a pogo-stick-hopping record to win some money.
Guest Stars: Nick, Joe and **Kevin Jonas** (collectively known as the **Jonas Brothers**) play themselves. The Jonas Brothers are recording artists, are tour-mates of Miley Cyrus on her Best of Both Worlds tour and are stars of the Disney Channel's original movie *Rock Camp*. Also, Disney Channel executives were so excited about the Jonas Brothers' appearance on *Hannah Montana* that they signed the trio to their own sitcom, *J.O.N.A.S.* (Junior Operatives Networking As Spies), and a reality show.

Highlight: When the Jonas Brothers are mad at Robby ("I shared my nachos with that guy!").

Did You Know?: This episode was the highest-rated episode for a cable television series, with 10.7 million viewers. The fake names that Miley and Lilly use are Milo and Otis, from a 1986 movie of the same name. Not only are they called the Jo Bros, Miley also calls them the Jonai, which is the plural form of Jonas in Latin. She also calls them Larry, Curly and Mo Bro, which are the names of The Three Stooges. The Stooges popularized slapstick comedy (based on stupid comments, and hitting each other), and in this episode, Joe and Kevin slap Nick whenever he says something stupid.

Did You Notice?: When the Jonai are fighting to get out the studio door, Nick is going out first, but when they switch the camera angle, Joe comes out first. Miley braids Lilly's hair, but then when the camera comes back to Lilly during Miley's fight with Robby, her hair is down, and then in the next shot, it's in a ponytail. When Jackson and Rico are dancing to "We Got the Party," Rico is on Jackson's shoulders, off his shoulder and then back on in the space of seven seconds.

Episode title inspired by: "Me and Mrs. Jones," recorded by Billy Paul

EPISODE 17: "Don't Stop Til You Get the Phone"
Original Air Date: September 21, 2007
When Robby won't buy her the new zPhone, Miley sells an embarrassing picture of Hannah Montana in order to buy one. Realizing that her necklace reveals Hannah is Miley, she makes a deal to trade the photo for a more embarrassing one of Dwayne "The Rock" Johnson. Meanwhile, Robby makes Jackson pay for ignoring his advice to wear sunscreen.

Highlight: The Rock in full make-up and curlers. (But who can resist the kitty cats lapping up the milk bath?!)

Guest Stars: **The Rock** plays himself. He is a wrestling superstar turned actor, who went from the WWE to starring in such films as *The Mummy Returns*, *The Scorpion King*, *Get Smart* and 2009's *Shazam!* His appearance was part of Disney Channel's "The Rock Block," which also included him guest-starring in an episode of *Cory in the House*. The Rock Block promotion for the Disney film *The Game Plan*, starring The Rock and Madison Pettis of *Cory in the House*, aired one week before the film premiered. Also, Leo, the guy from the *National Inquiry*, was played by **Tom McGowan**, a regular from the TV shows *Frasier* and *Everybody Loves Raymond*.

Did You Know?: The episode is inspired by the phone marketing campaigns of 2007. Apple introduced its iPhone in summer 2007, less than three months before the episode aired. Traci's zPhone looks to be a decorated BlackBerry smartphone, the iPhone's main

competition. Also, in another twist on not using brands, Robby and Jackson declare themselves fans of Tennessee football, but never use the name of the NFL team, the Titans. Robby even wears the jersey of star Titans running back Eddie George (#27), but the name "Titans" is blacked out.

Did You Notice?: When Hannah shakes Lola's head, the oPhone disappears from Lola's left hand. Although Miley only bought her "Miley" necklace just last week, she wore it earlier in the "Achey Jakey Heart, Part 2" episode, just after the opening credits.

Episode title inspired by: "Don't Stop Til You Get Enough," recorded by Michael Jackson

EPISODE 18: "That's What Friends Are For?"
Original Air Date: October 19, 2007
Jake Ryan returns and asks Miley to be friends. But then he starts shooting a movie with Mikayla, Hannah's rival. Miley convinces Lilly to help get Mikayla fired from the movie, but they are found out. So Miley has to apologize to everyone involved. Meanwhile, Rico bets

Jackson and Oliver to go without using water for a few days.

Guest Star: Selena Gomez returns as Mikayla.

Highlight: When Jake Ryan walks out, and then walks back in to make up with Miley as friends.

Did You Know?: Jake Ryan plays Roger Bucks, Intergalactic Bounty Hunter, an allusion to Buck Rogers, a sci-fi hero from a 1970s TV series and earlier. *The Real Deal with Colin Lassiter* shoots in Studio 2 of the same company that shoots *Wake Up, It's Wendy* in Studio 4. Colin Lassiter is back again. He's played by Michael Kagan who was on a couple of episodes of *Suddenly Susan*, which *Hannah's* Steve Peterman produced.

Did You Notice?: When Miley returns from the charity telethon, the purple jacket and the Hannah wig keep moving places on her arm, depending on the take. When Robby picks up the dead seagull, it has moved places and its wingspan is much wider. And why are Miley and Lilly at Jake's taping of *Wake Up, It's Wendy*?

Episode title inspired by: "That's What Friends Are For," recorded by Dionne Warwick

EPISODE 19: "Lilly's Mom Has Got it Goin' On"

Original Air Date: November 9, 2007

Miley and Lilly are thrilled when Robby and Lilly's mom go out on a date. But when there's an argument over who pays the bill, each daughter defends her parent. The fight goes on until there's a battle over a bucket of fish at school, and both realize it's not their fight. Meanwhile, Rico bets Jackson he couldn't be the boss for the weekend, which gets Jackson into trouble.

Guest Star: Heather Locklear plays Heather Truscott, Lilly's mom. Heather has had a long career in television since 1979. Among the shows she has been a regular on are *Dynasty*, *T.J. Hooker*, *Melrose Place*, *Spin City* and, most recently, *LAX*. Heather was convinced to guest star after she attended a taping of *Hannah Montana* with her kids.

Highlight: The fish fight, especially the end when Okenland is dragged back into the classroom by Saratopia.

Did You Know?: All of the PTA parents bring vegetarian dishes to the meeting; Miley Cyrus is a vegetarian . . . who doesn't eat any green vegetables! Miley Cyrus's best friend Mandy is one of her back-up dancers, and she appears in this episode. It was directed by Jody Margolin Hahn, who directed two other episodes this season. Roger S. Christiansen again directed most of the episodes so far this season (thirteen), and the other directors were Rich Correll (four episodes), Mark Cendrowski (two) and Sean Lambert (one).

Did You Notice?: Mr. Corelli (played by Greg Baker) is Miley's drama teacher in the eighth grade ("Oh Say, Can You Remember the Words?"), her history teacher in the ninth grade ("I Am Hannah, Hear Me Croak") and her geography teacher in this episode. Lilly's mom, Heather, must also know the Hannah/Miley secret; she's wearing a disguise like Lilly's.

Episode title inspired by: "Stacy's Mom," recorded by The Fountains of Wayne

EPISODE 20: "I Will Always Loathe You"

Original Air Date: December 7, 2007

Mamaw Ruthie and Aunt Dolly come to town to watch Miley get an international music award, and they start feuding again, because Dolly stole Elvis from Ruthie in high school. When they fight each other at the awards show, Miley has to teach them about forgiveness. Meanwhile, Oliver helps Rico cast a commercial for the shack.

Guest Stars: Vicki Lawrence returns as Mamaw Ruthie, and **Dolly Parton** returns as Aunt Dolly.

Highlight: Mamaw and Dolly shadow-fighting (although when Dolly is whipping Mamaw around, it looks too much like a rag doll).

Did You Know?: The actor who plays Rico's brother is Mateo Arias, Moises's real brother. This episode was written by Michael Poryes. Both he and Douglas Lieblein each wrote four episodes so far this season, while Andrew Green, Heather Wordham and Sally Lapiduss each wrote three.

Did You Notice?: In the cabinet beside the kitchen, there's a paddle with an 8 on it, which looks like one of the paddles from *Dancing With the Stars*. Billy Ray was always hoping for an 8. Robby goes from being Hannah's security guy in the first episode, to being her manager, and then her songwriter, and now everyone knows Hannah's father is the once-famous Robby Ray Stewart? How can Hannah have a secret identity if this keeps up?

Episode title inspired by: "I Will Always Love You," recorded by Dolly Parton and Whitney Houston

EPISODE 21: "Bye-Bye, Ball"

Original Air Date: January 13, 2008

When Jackson accidentally destroys Beary, Miley gets revenge destroying his baseball signed by Joey Vitolo. But when Jackson fixes Beary, Miley visits Vitolo's to get a new signed ball. However, because his daughter is a Hannah fan, Hannah has to return to get the signed ball. But Joey wants to sing duets with her, and push the veal. Jackson arrives to let her off the hook.

Guest Star: Joey Fatone plays Joey Vitolo. Joey was a member of the boy band *N Sync, contestant on *Dancing With the Stars* (the same season as Billy Ray) and actor in a number of films, including *On the Line*, *My Big Fat Greek Wedding* and *The Cooler*. He served as host of NBC's *Spelling Bee* and appeared on stage in *Rent* and *Little Shop of Horrors*.

Highlight: Jackson interrogating Oliver and Lilly, and to break him, putting Oliver into his closet.

Did You Know?: Justin Timberlake and Joey Fatone were bandmates in *N Sync, which is why Jackson has the line about a Timberlake mask. Joey and Hannah's dance at the end of the episode has some similar moves to *N Sync's "Bye Bye Bye" choreography. Robby alludes to being in *Dancing With the Stars* with Joey, when he says, "If I could dance like him, I'd give myself a ten."

Did You Notice?: Before Jackson swats at the wasp with Beary, you can see the rip in Beary's bottom when it's on Miley's lap. When Miley and Lilly are in Jackson's room, they leave the muscle body with Jackson's head lying on the floor, but when Jackson returns to find a shirt, it's not there anymore.

Episode title inspired by: "Bye Bye Bye," recorded by *N Sync

EPISODE 22: "(We're So Sorry) Uncle Earl"

Original Air Date: March 21, 2008

Uncle Earl visits the Stewarts on a quest to become a rock star, just as critic Barney Bittman is reviewing a Hannah concert. When Earl causes the lead guitarist's hand to break, he steps in. Although Jackson does his Ozzy-best to lure Barney away, Earl learns of Hannah's embarrassment. Yet Hannah asks him to play, and Barney loves his classic-rock playing.

Guest Stars: David Koechner plays Uncle Earl. David's first big movie role was as Champ Kind in *Anchorman*, and he's been in dozens of movies, including the starring role in *The Comebacks*. He also starred in the TV series *The Naked Trucker* and *T-Bones Show* and had a recurring role on *The Office*. **Gilbert Gottfried** plays Barney Bittman. Gilbert is best known for his voice work in cartoons, especially as the parrot in Disney's *Aladdin*, and has appeared in many movies and TV shows.

Highlight: When Jackson hears the *Hannah Montana* theme on the TV, he yells, "When is this not on?" Also Cuddles the pig, and his tinkle box.

Did You Know?: Robby says he had the sexiest unibrow in Beaufort County, but there isn't any such county in Tennessee (but there is one in neighboring North Carolina).

Did You Notice?: Robby is the only guitarist in Hannah's band (the other's playing bass guitar), and his playing doesn't match the music. Miley came out to the porch after her first concert, which means the Stewarts bought the house in Malibu before Hannah Montana was famous.

Episode title inspired by: "Uncle Albert/Admiral Halsey," recorded by Paul McCartney and Wings

EPISODE 23: "The Way We Almost Weren't"

On tour, Miley and Jackson want to rush home. Robby wants to stop at an old café, and tell them a story. Miley almost gets hit by lightning, and the kids find themselves in 1987 at this same café where their parents first met, but this time they're not meeting. As Jackson fades away, Miley finds a way for their parents' eyes to meet. Meanwhile, Lilly and Oliver get glued to a couple of Rico's chairs.

Guest Star: Brooke Shields is back as Miley's mom in 1987.

Highlight: The waitress serving the Stewarts niblets every time they say, "Sweet niblets!"

Did You Know?: Miley's mom, Susan, is listening on her headphones to "Walk Like An Egyptian," a song recorded by The Bangles that hit #1 in December 1986 (the flashback is June 1987). The oldest disappearing first when history gets changed was the way it worked in *Back to the Future*, the hit film from 1985.

Did You Notice?: The lipstick smear on Miley's face changes from shot to shot. The exte-

rior shot of the café has cars from the '70s. When Jackson goes to the washroom, he goes left, but later on, a man comes from the right. In the episode "Good Golly, Miss Dolly," Aunt Dolly says that Miley's mom turned Robby down when he first asked her out, but in this episode they talk all night at the diner after looking into each other's eyes.
Episode title inspired by: "The Way We Were" recorded by Barbra Streisand

EPISODE 24: "We're All On This Date Together"
Hannah, Lola and Mike Standley attend a celebrity auction. When two bids for a date with Hannah tie, she agrees to go out with both winning bidders — Johnny Collins and Rico. Rico gets a cold from Lilly and Oliver, but he goes on the date anyway. Hannah treats him so poorly, that Johnny leaves.
Guest Stars: Corbin Bleu returns as Johnny Collins, whom Miley crushed in the first episode of *Hannah Montana.* **Donny Osmond** plays the auctioneer. Donny said in a recent interview that appeaaring on a Disney Channel show brings his career full circle since he and his family first sang professionally at Disneyland. Singing with the Osmond Brothers led to a solo singing career for Donny in the early 1970s. He and his sister Marie had a hit variety show in the late 1970s, and he starred in musical theater and films throughout the last two decades. **Ray Romano** is one of the celebrities at the auction (a day with Ray fetches less than a date with Hannah). Ray was a stand-up comic before hitting it big witht the TV series, *Everybody Loves Raymond.* He also voiced Manny the Mammoth in the *Ice Age* movies.
Highlight: Rico in the lobster tank.
Did You Know?: Donny Osmond (who also comes from a faith-based showbiz family, and hit it big at age fourteen) had exclusive access at the *Best of Both Worlds* movie premiere for *ET,* including a one-on-one interview with Miley during which the set fell down.
Episode title inspired by: "We're All In This Together," the closing song from *High School Musical*

★

For more *Hannah Montana* episode guides and the latest in the Miley Cyrus News Diary, check out **ecwpress.com/hannahmiley**

★